how the other half lives

HOW THE OTHER HALF LIVES

The Challenges Facing Clergy Spouses and Partners

Johnna Fredrickson and William Smith

THE PILGRIM PRESS
CLEVELAND

FOR Dave, Colin, and Jared—the home team. For Cheri and Elizabeth, the world's greatest conversation partners. For all spouses and partners, lay and ordained: this book would not be possible without you. —J.F.

TO William and Elizabeth for providing the foundation, and Larry, Barbara, and Sheila for providing the inspiration and mentorship. —W.S.

The Pilgrim Press, 700 Prospect Avenue, Cleveland, Ohio 44115-1100
thepilgrimpress.com

Printed in the United States of America on acid-free paper

14 13 12 11 10 5 4 3 2 1

Library of Congress Cataloging-in-Publication Data

Fredrickson, Johnna, 1964–
How the other half lives : the challenges facing clergy spouses and partners / Johnna Fredrickson and William Smith.
p. cm.
Includes bibliographical references.
ISBN 978-0-8298-1872-7 (acid-free paper)
1. Spouses of clergy I. Smith, William, A.M. II. Title.
BV4395.F66 2010
253'.22—dc22 2010022160

CONTENTS

PREFACE

Taking the Ministry Plunge

This book is for those who find themselves in marriage and union with clergymen and -women. There are other books. Some provide a very particular model of the "minister's wife" or "clergy spouse." Some seem to promote a Ward and June Cleaver lifestyle, with a church on the side and Ward in a collar. Quite a few assume that the minister has a wife, not a husband; this was valid a few decades ago, but no longer. Some are sweet, some boring, a few are angry. Many are merely collections of anecdotes, incidents from the lives of the spouses of the religiously employed. This is not that kind of a book.

Being a clergy spouse or partner is complicated. For some, it is the most wonderful and demanding way to live out a relationship with a life partner and with God. For others, it is always coming in last place behind spiritual crises, marriages, births, deaths, and worship services. Some spouses find strong support and life-giving friendships with the people in the faith communities that employ their other half. Others are shunted to the side, always an appendage to their partner, never seen as individuals with their own value. For most, navigating the waters of faith and a committed personal relationship with a clergyman or clergywoman requires a great deal of energy, effort, and nerve. This book is a chart of the waters, deep and shallow, with notes from those who sail them.

The chapters of this book review many issues that spouses and their clergy halves encounter. Chapter 1 sets the stage by reminding both partners that all people stand equal before God, and that all ministries are worked out within the union or marriage of the couple. Ordained ministry is a particular way to live out a call to serve God, but it is no more or less holy than other ways. Chapter 2 focuses on the church community: what are the issues facing spouses who worship in the communities that their husbands and wives lead? What happens to partners who choose to join a different faith community?

Chapters 3 and 4 are quite practical. The third chapter centers on how ministry affects the working life of a clergy spouse or partner. Whose career takes priority? How does relocation affect work life and advancement? Because clergy are rarely overpaid, the work life of the spouse or partner may be necessary to cover basic expenses. Chapter 4 introduces the host of housing possibilities that face clergy families. The benefits and drawbacks of owning a home and of living in church-owned housing are reviewed.

Chapter 5 explores the life-giving practice of rest. Keeping time apart for rest and rejuvenation, for play and prayer, helps keep a clergy couple and family connected to God and each other—and may just keep everyone sane.

Chapter 6 addresses the many aspects of marriage from a marriage studies perspective and from a therapist's perspective. What are the major issues that face all couples? What helps relationships grow and what damages them?

The seventh chapter centers on children and how the ordained ministry of a parent affects their lives. When a clergy parent takes a call, children must adjust to new communities, new schools, and new faith communities. Life can be complex for Preachers' Kids.

What is the foundation of a faith life? How is God's grace found in the many experiences of clergy spouses and partners? What if the whole thing falls apart? Chapter 8 is the final word of faith.

At the end of the book is a list of resources that may be helpful for clergy spouses and partners. Also included is a survey for spouses and partners that is part of ongoing research, and directions for those who would like to participate in this research.

Most people reading this book are clergy spouses and partners—or men and women who soon will be. For this reason, and because one of the writers is a clergy spouse, this book is from a spouse's point of view and written to other partners and spouses. Others may also find this book interesting or helpful, including clergy, pastoral counselors, ordination committee members, and practical theologians. For all who venture into its pages, may it be well worth the time and effort it takes to get from here to the end.

Introductory Words

THE BEGINNING OF IT ALL

[I]n your baptism you have been called to union with Christ and the church. Do you intend to honor this calling through the covenant of marriage?[1]

God of mercy, your faithfulness to your covenant frees us to live together in the security of your powerful love. Amid all the changing words of our generation, speak your eternal Word that does not change. Then may we respond to your gracious promises by living in faith and obedience; through our Lord Jesus Christ. Amen. . . .

[S]ince it is your intention to marry, join your right hands, and with your promises bind yourselves to each other as husband and wife.[2]

Eternal God, . . . [g]ive them wisdom and devotion in the ordering of their common life, that each may be to the other a strength in need, a counselor in perplexity, a comfort in sorrow, and a companion in joy. Amen.

Grant that their wills may be so knit together in your will, and their spirits in your Spirit, that they may grow in love and peace with you and one another all the days of their life. Amen.

Give them grace, when they hurt each other, to recognize and acknowledge their fault, and to seek each other's forgiveness and yours. Amen.

Make their life together a sign of Christ's love to this sinful and broken world, that unity may overcome estrangement, forgiveness heal guilt, and joy conquer despair. Amen.

Bestow on them, if it is your will, the gift and heritage of children, and the grace to bring them up to know you, to love you, and to serve you. Amen.

Give them such fulfillment of their mutual affection that they may reach out in love and concern for others. Amen. . . .

Grant that the bonds of our common humanity, by which all your children are united to one another, and the living to the dead, may be so transformed by your grace, that your will may be done on earth as it is in heaven; where, O Father, with your Son and the Holy Spirit, you live and reign in perfect unity, now and forever. Amen.[3]

❖

WRECKONCILIATION, by Rev. David R. Anderson[4]

Joy scheduled never arrives.

It was to be a weekend away, something pastors rarely get. Pam and I had tickets to the Museum of Modern Art in the city, and reservations at Danny Myer's Modern for lunch on Friday. Then it was on to Philadelphia to have dinner with friends in their new apartment. Saturday would be late breakfast, a day to savor Philadelphia again after a long absence.

We never did it. Oh, we showed up at all those places, but in deep conflict.

It started on Tuesday night. I came home for dinner and announced that I was going to a meeting, when usually Tuesdays are kept free of evening engagements. Pam already had an evening planned. Sorry, I said, this one was unavoidable. That wasn't cutting it. She needed more from me, and she was not asking. She was insisting.

I returned from my Tuesday night meeting to find Pam in bed, awake, staring at the wall. I got in on my side and stared at the ceiling.

In the morning we went through the motions of morning prayer and then for our regular run. We tried to talk but engagement turned to accusation. I turned around and ran home.

On Wednesday and Thursday we spoke on an as-needed basis. We both assumed we would work it out this weekend, when we had all that time. But come Friday we struggled to get our work done and out the door. Frustration hardened our separate positions. The roots of this hostility were clearly wrapped around deep, unresolved conflicts.

Driving through the gray, wintry landscape, I refused to talk. Pam broke the silence and I declined to reciprocate. I was hurt. I was angry. I felt misunderstood. I thought of the profoundly intimate talks we shared just a few weeks ago, of—frankly—the good husband I knew I had been. But I refused to make my case. Like Walter Mitty, I preferred to take my hits and suffer this outrageous traducement in noble silence.

I think that for a man, a long car ride with a woman in conflict is hell. He cannot get away. If he were home, he could walk out—go watch badminton on ESPN, slam the door and walk anywhere. But in the car, there is nowhere to run. She can ask him to talk about the problem, and if he declines she can wait 10 minutes and ask him to talk about why he feels this way. If this fails, she can start talking to herself, to the windshield. And then, before long, he is talking about why he's not talking about it, and that is a slippery slope to reconciliation.

A few years ago, we brought a male cat into a home where a female cat was queen. We thought she would take the kitty and mother it, but she rebuffed his early advances and he took to ambushing her from behind the sofa.

The vet suggested this: Put them both under a laundry basket and leave them there in that awfully confined space until they learned to accept each other's inescapable presence. We tried it once or twice, but they escaped and then, once they knew the plot, it was impossible to catch them again.

It may never work for cats. I don't know. It worked once, though, for two humans.

MEMO: "WRECKONCILIATION" by Pam Anderson[5]

To: David
From: Pam
Re.: "Wreckonciliation"

OK. So I did give you permission to run that article in *Tidings* a few weeks ago. After I read it, you offered to change it, rewrite it even, but there was a side of me that rather liked it. In return, however, I've asked for equal time.

First, I appreciate your honesty and openness—as a man, a clergyman at that. I've long felt we families of the cloth have to act like we've got it all together. We don't, of course. We curse, fight, struggle with money, have problems with our kids, get depressed, battle vices, and face mid-life crises like everybody else.

Publicly acknowledging our imperfections is scary and powerful—scary because we're supposed to be the ideal family. If we don't have it together, then there's no hope for everyone else. On the other hand, if we can honestly share our struggles and triumphs, I think we offer true hope for others. Which brings me to Tuesday, January 31, the night you had a meeting and I got mad.

You accurately portrayed our conflict, but you made it seem that I got upset because of this one little, unavoidable meeting on an isolated Tuesday night. You didn't mention you were the one who decided last fall that you weren't scheduling meetings on Tuesday and Thursday evenings. (By the way, let the record show that as I'm writing this on Tuesday night, February 28, you, my friend, are at a meeting.)

The no-meetings-on-Tuesday-and-Thursday-nights rule was your recent response to years of my frustration. You work for the church, yet our family has never had a sacred time—a moment that only emergencies could interrupt. For a long time I accepted it. How could I question God's work? He trumped me every time.

Then you came up with this new plan. These sacred nights weren't necessarily family time, although an occasional movie would be nice. They were mostly for you—to read *The New Yorker,* keep in touch with our finances, read (or write!) a novel, help plan our daughter's wedding—anything but work.

In just a few short months, however, you had already made so many exceptions that your scheduling meetings on those nights seemed like no big deal. And here's the kicker. After that Tuesday night meeting, you slipped over to the office and worked another hour before coming home.

That was the deep-seated conflict you alluded to in your article. Yes, the car ride was painfully hard work. The script was old and tired; we knew our parts by heart. When you went mute, though, I thought you didn't care, which is why I was so persistent. I needed to know.

I got my answer. Since that trip and the tentative days that followed, we're living a bit differently. Yes, there was that Tuesday night meeting this week, but after the last Ash Wednesday service, you bolted out of the sacristy before I could even finish talking with friends. When we got home, you heated up the pasta, grabbed my hand and said, "Let's watch a movie."

ONE

In the Beginning, Baptism

All baptized Christians are called to ministry. It springs from the Holy Spirit's presence with them. The gifts of every believer are gifts for living in love with God and neighbor, and for deepening the spiritual lives of all. The apostle Paul puts it this way:

> Now there are a variety of gifts, but the same Spirit; and there are varieties of services, but the same Lord; and there are varieties of activities, but it is the same God who activates all of them in everyone. To each is given the manifestation of the Spirit for the common good . . . All these are activated by one and the same Spirit, who allots to each one individually just as the Spirit chooses. (1 Cor. 12:4–7)

When a child or adult is baptized, it is not just to spend a life sitting in a pew and being an upright member of the community. All believers are:

- Sent into the world in witness to God's love
- Received into the household of God
- Charged to confess the faith of Christ crucified, proclaim his resurrection, and share in his eternal priesthood[1]
- Joined to Christ's ministry of love, peace, and justice
- Charged to fulfill the calling to be a disciple of Jesus Christ
- Sealed by the Holy Spirit

- Marked as Christ's own forever
- Grafted into Christ forever
- Made members of the household of God, to share in the priesthood of Christ with others[2]

These baptismal truths are reaffirmed for some at confirmation, and reaffirmed for all when participating in the baptism of another within the faith community. All baptized Christians have gifts, and all stand as equals in faith before God. There are no first tier and second tier Christians, set apart by the Spirit's favor and professional demeanor: there are only Christians with different gifts and different ways to live out God's love. Whatever work is done—waiting tables, driving school buses, caring for the sick, leading a church—can be done to God's glory, a sure sign of the Spirit's myriad gifts and of God's love. There are some people who live God's holiness more fully serving coffee than others do serving as chaplains or preachers. There are ordained ministers who are saintly and teachers who are cruel. Living a life of faith and love is about living into Christ's love for others most honestly. A saintly life isn't about having a particular profession, but about living into daily work with humility and compassion. Doing dishes with a sense of holiness is as godly as preaching to the multitude if it is done as a baptismal calling.

That's all well and good until someone moves from a baptismal ministry to an ordained one. Suddenly, the word "call" comes into the dialogue about faith and work in a way that it rarely does otherwise. Few would say that they are "called" by God to be social workers, librarians, bookkeepers, and bakers—even when it is the profound truth!

WHEN BAPTISMAL MINISTRY BECOMES A PROFESSIONAL CALLING

Hearing a call to serve Christ as an ordained minister is one way for the gifts of the Spirit to be lived out fully. It is not the only way, but the one way that comes to mind if someone mentions being "called" to a particular vocation. In a previous version (2006) of its ordination handbook, the Episcopal Diocese of Massachusetts put it this way:

> Academic accomplishment, a life of caring and compassion, a history of personal struggle and courage, a strong sense of personal

> call—all of these are valuable, but not of themselves evidence of a call to ordination . . . it is time to put to rest the notion that ordination recognizes those who are more spiritual than others.[3]

The handbook goes on to talk about a call to ordination being one for those who are able to lead the faith community in living out its mission—to serve God in the world and enable believers to participate in God's love by serving others. Professional ordained ministry is not a measure of faithfulness, or spirituality, but a particular way some are called to live their lives of faith. Ordained ministry is neither a greater nor lesser way to live a godly life: it is the way that some will live a godly life most fully. There is no spiritual judgment involved with the spiritual discernment of call to ordination unless it is either sought or rejected outside of the baptismal call to serve God. The ordained and the nonordained (lay) stand as equals before God, living lives equally faithful and equally unfaithful. Sadly, this truth often remains closed within the ordination manuals of the various denominations, out of reach for spouses and partners.

If ordination and full-time ministry are not the highest forms of spiritual life, then what are they? Simply put, they are ways to live out a faith life most deeply for some. For others, this is not true, just as creating stained glass is not the best way of living in faith for all people. Certain people have gifts for ministry, gifts given to them by the Holy Spirit for serving God through the church. In *Primary Qualities for Professional Ministry*, a resource for the Presbyterian Church (USA), six crucial qualities are:

- Lives in relationship with God
- Lives in relationship with self
- Lives in relationship with others
- Has communication and leadership potential/skills
- Has an inquiring creative orientation toward life
- Can make commitments and carry out responsibilities[4]

The Episcopal Diocese of Massachusetts lists these qualities as crucial for those called to ordained ministry:

- If Jesus Christ is the source of hope and joy for you,
- If you see a world hungry for Christ's healing love,
- If you are able to gather, teach, and inspire other people,
- If you can make peace between people in conflict,
- If you meet the living God in Anglican worship,
- If you are nourished by prayer and the sacraments,
- If you are devoted to God's Word in Holy Scripture,
- If you help others find God in times of grief or anguish,
- If you are willing to sacrifice many comforts to do Christ's work,
- If you are able to seek and serve Christ in all people,
- If you seek opportunities to create, build, and transform,
- If your church community has identified these qualities in you, you may be called to serve as a deacon or priest in the Diocese of Massachusetts.[5]

In the United Church of Christ, the following qualities are desired in those seeking to be ministers:

- A healthy sense of self as shaped by God, community, and personal experience.
- A sense of theological identity and authority, while being responsive to the opinions and values of others, including those whom the Member (minister) will serve.
- A healthy awareness of strengths, weaknesses, and limits, and assumption of responsibility for one's body, mind, and spirit.
- Knowledge and observance of personal and professional boundaries in interpersonal, congregational, and community settings.[6]

The UCC lists these five points as the spiritual foundation for ministry:

- A lived faith showing love of God, trust in Jesus, and openness to the Holy Spirit.
- Devotion to the word of God as revealed through scripture and Christian traditions.

- Commitment to lifelong spiritual growth and practice, individually and in community.
- A sense of being called by God and the community to authorized ministry in the church.
- Openness to continuing discernment of one's call in community.[7]

Other denominations have similar lists, all designed to help individuals and the committees that oversee them affirm a call to ordination or question its validity. But there are other things in these guides, things that are less positive and less about the individual's inner faith. The implications of full-time ministry for all involved are ever so briefly touched upon. The reality isn't pretty.

> The work of ordained ministry can be exhilarating and joyful, and the joy can include members of the deacon's or priest's immediate family. It can also be a source of strain, confusion, and sometimes anger. The Bishop and the Commission [on Ministry of the Episcopal Diocese of Massachusetts] urge everyone who considers ordination to include spouses, partners, and families in the discernment process from the very first. We strongly recommend conversation with professional counselors and with experienced members of the clergy.[8]

Why such tension? The demands of professional ministry are many and often ill-defined. Discerning a call to ordination is an individual affair in many ways because it is that individual person who will be ordained. At the same time, his or her relationships, including the one with a spouse or partner, are profoundly affected. Lives are turned around. Those closest to ministers sometimes feel like they are spinning out of control in this ministry centrifuge. Ministers must be "tolerant of long hours, misunderstandings, irrational love and hostility."[9] How can such things not affect marriages and unions? While ordination guides are written for those going through the ordination process, those who accompany need and deserve guidance. With some thought and preparation, partners and spouses can prepare themselves as passengers on the long, bumpy journey into ordained ministry reality. Without it, the reality of living in relationship to clergywomen and clergymen may leave spouses and partners disoriented to the point of spiritual motion sickness. As with most trips, the best place to start is at the beginning. The first place on the map is at the root of the call to ordination: biblical accounts of God calling men and women to serve.

BIBLICAL IMAGES OF GOD'S CALL

When thinking of biblical accounts of God calling individuals to service, one of the most notable is Jesus calling the disciples.

> As he walked by the Sea of Galilee, he saw two brothers, Simon, who is called Peter, and Andrew his brother, casting a net into the sea—for they were fishermen. And he said to them, "Follow me, and I will make you fish for people." Immediately they left their nets and followed him. As he went from there, he saw two brothers, James son of Zebedee, and his brother John, in the boat with their father Zebedee, mending their nets, and he called them. Immediately they left the boat and their father, and followed him. (Matthew 4:18–22)[10]

When Jesus calls Peter, Andrew, James, and John, they leave their boats behind to follow him. There seems to be no turning back, no saying good-bye, and apparently no thought to the loved ones left in the boat or at home. Does a call to serve Jesus mean that everyone and everything can and must be left behind? Is this a "get out of family responsibility free" card? What about those left holding the nets and waiting at home?

Undoubtedly, there are those who feel that a call to follow Jesus is a call to leave everything and everyone behind, that serving God in Christ's church means giving up all vestiges of a former life. But this interpretation of Jesus calling the disciples is not the only one. Once again, it depends upon what "call" means.

In his commentary on the Gospel of Matthew, Douglas R. A. Hare writes that the way the disciples answer the call to follow Jesus is not truly about their futures as disciples, but represents "all future believers whom Jesus irresistibly summons to follow him. It may not be necessary for all to leave professions and possessions behind, but all must leave their world behind and enter a new world into which Jesus invites them."[11] Plainly put, all faithful people leave behind who they were in order to become who they are in Christ. This is not the story of a call to professional ministry, but the story of how Jesus calls all people to follow him. This is the call for everyone to live out his or her baptismal ministry. Some may change careers and some may not, but no one will be the same after answering Jesus' call. Jesus summons everyone to follow, giving everyone the opportunity to live lives transformed by his love.

Getting out of the boat is not about changing a career, although that may happen: getting out of the boat is about doing whatever work is done in a way that shows Christ's love for others. No partner or spouse need be left behind in the boat, holding the shredded nets of pre-ordination life, because the call is not about a profession. Lives will be changed when Jesus calls. How these lives will be transformed cannot be predicted, only lived out. But all who answer the call to follow step out of the boat on equal footing. How a spouse or partner lives out a life of following Jesus may not be as obvious, but when done in faith and love is just as valuable.

In Judges, there is an account of Deborah's call to serve God. It is an ancient story about a remarkable woman called to be the leader of God's people in a time and culture that assumed men would be the political and religious leaders.

> At that time Deborah, a prophetess, wife of Lappidoth, was judging Israel. She used to sit under the palm of Deborah between Ramah and Bethel in the hill country of Ephraim; and the Israelites came to her for judgment. . . . Then Deborah got up and went with Barak. . . . (Judges 4:4ff.)

In ancient Israel, a judge was not merely someone who settled legal disputes. Deborah was the chieftain, responsible for political leadership in peace and war. As a prophetess, she was also a religious leader. In *The New Jerome Biblical Commentary*, M. O'Connor notes that the task of the judges was to bring God's will to bear upon the lives of the people, leading them into a deeper relationship with God and insuring their continued prosperity through obedience to God's wishes.[12]

Deborah is the only woman called by God to be a judge over the tribes of Israel. Women were not usually in positions of power, but when selected by God could assume leadership roles. When Deborah became a judge and went to war with the military leader, Barak, both she and her husband were put into unfamiliar roles. When the one who traditionally works in the private sphere of the family becomes a political and religious leader, does the spouse assume the duties of the household? Did Lappidoth and Deborah switch duties, or were the usual duties and roles suspended in favor of new and different ways of negotiating family and work responsibilities? What did that do to their relationship as wife and husband?

Unlike the account of the disciples getting out of the boat and leaving family behind, there is no clear departure for Deborah when she becomes a judge. She is identified as the wife of Lappidoth rather than removed from marriage. After becoming a judge, Deborah does go to war with Barak, but it is unclear whether she returned to her home, family, and life as a judge when the battles ceased. Deborah's identity as a religious leader is not removed from her husband. There are no accounts of how Deborah and Lappidoth worked out their union in connection with their faith and her call to be a community spiritual leader. It seems that a call to serve God as a professional does not guarantee an easy or obvious way of being in a covenant relationship, just a life lived in the richness of God's love and service.

What were the expectations that the community had for Deborah and Lappidoth? Was it more difficult for Lappidoth to be a "clergy" spouse because he was a man? The lack of a definite description of how Deborah and Lappidoth lived leaves room for imagining what a faithful marriage might be in light of someone's call to ordained ministry. Lappidoth's story remains private, Deborah's role as religious leader and spouse ambiguous. In this very ambiguity, the clergy marriages and unions of today may find a biblical counterpart. There is some breathing room here, a space to live faithfully into a new way of being in relationship.

In the two Bible passages just reviewed, individuals answer the call to follow God by leaving behind a work life. The disciples gave up fishing and Deborah left the private realm of her family to faithfully serve God. What if both partners are called?

> After this, Paul left Athens and went to Corinth. There he found a Jew named Aquila, a native of Pontus, who had recently come from Italy with his wife Priscilla, because Claudius had ordered all Jews to leave Rome. Paul went to see them, and, because he was of the

> same trade, he stayed with them, and they worked together—by trade they were tentmakers. . . . After staying there for a considerable time, Paul said farewell to the believers and sailed for Syria, accompanied by Priscilla and Aquila. At Cenchreae he had his hair cut, for he was under a vow. When they reached Ephesus, he left them there. (Acts 18:1–3, 18–19)

The apostle Paul meets Priscilla and Aquila in Corinth. He remains with them, working with them as tentmakers. All three serve the church and eventually move to Ephesus. Aquila and Priscilla are left there to lead the community of faith while Paul moves on. Most likely, the couple continued to support themselves as tentmakers while serving as church leaders.

Because both Priscilla and Aquila are mentioned by name, it is likely that they were both leaders within the church, working as equal partners and accompanying Paul on his missionary journey. In his commentary on Acts, William H. Willimon notes that Priscilla is listed first as they go to Ephesus, implying that she was a leader of the church equal to Aquila or above him in stature.[13] Willimon also points out that Paul's emphasis on his work as a tentmaker shows a high regard for lay labor. Priscilla and Aquila not only witness to God's love and goodness by serving as church worship leaders, but by the way they live their whole lives personally and professionally.

In Aquila and Priscilla, we find a couple united in both their lay work as tentmakers and in their roles within the Christian faith community. Converted to the faith at some point, both share a call to serve Christ, working out their marriage in its context. Equally important is the reverse: their calls to serve Christ are worked out within the context of their covenant relationship with one another. Relationships to each other and to God are lived out simultaneously, each integral to them as individuals and as a couple. The emphasis on the whole life of believers being the true witness gives continuity to the work and evangelism of this couple. Their personal identities as Christians and their professional identities as tentmakers and church leaders come together, transformed by faith and worked out in mutual relationship. In their case, no one is left in the boat or tending the business while the "called" one leaves all things behind. What is left behind is a life lived in separation from faith in Christ. It seems that Priscilla and Aquila work out their individual faith lives within the context of their mutual covenant relationship. Neither one is the appendage or shadow of the other, but their mutual faith and labor provide the context for their individual growth.

BRINGING IT ALL TOGETHER

Several different elements have come into play in this exploration of life as a clergy partner or spouse—biblical accounts of call, promises made in marriage and union ceremonies, and seeking to live a life of faith. How do these come together in a way that helps clergy spouses and partners navigate the difficulties that come with clergy life?

The first element is the marriage or union promises that bind two individuals to each other and to the life of faith.[14] Promises are made to honor one another and to live lives of faith not as separate individuals, but as members of a covenant relationship. Who each person is as an individual develops alongside the other, leading to mutual growth in faith. Both are equal before God, both choose to live out their baptismal callings in constant relationship with the other. This is not an invitation to become a single entity, with one overwhelming the other, but an invitation to be fully oneself while in communion with another. One partner cannot erase the needs and gifts of the other; one cannot demand the space to grow as an individual without granting that space to his or her spouse.

The covenant of Christian marriage or union is not only a promise between two people concerning their private lives. It is equally a sign of connection to the larger faith community. The promises are made in the context of baptism, which is a profound connection with all other Christians. All are joined together in Christ through baptism, remaining connected throughout life. Faith ties the couple together and anchors them securely in the larger community. Through marriage and union, the love of Christ shines. A marriage is nurtured through its connection with the larger community, just as community life is enriched by the grace of those who are bound together in union. The marriage finds a strong foundation in faith and becomes the way in which two people are drawn more deeply into God's love for them and for the world. Each individual is connected to the other and to the larger faith community, and held in God's love. The interconnections among the individuals, the couple together, and the larger community are all transformed by God's grace, allowing Christ's presence to be manifested in ever deeper ways.

With a call to ordained and full-time ministry, the balance of the marriage or union is challenged. The two individuals find that their vision of what their common life would be is changed. Whether they entered into covenant relationship before or after one of them felt called to ordained ministry, the marriage or union will face challenges that are not a part of the lives of nonclergy couples. Many couples feel that their private lives are no longer private. Their actions and relationship are up for public scrutiny within the faith community and beyond. When a call to serve a church or other ministry is taken, both may lose a faith community in the relocation. Many feel pressure to present a façade of relational perfection, which saps the energy of both partners. For some spouses, their own faith lives are demoted to an extension of their partner's public ministry and personal faith. It is in the face of this reality that the biblical stories of call can provide alternate ways of living a relationship as a couple and as individuals of faith.

When Jesus calls the disciples to follow, they leave work and family behind. This is not a paradigm for answering a call to professional ministry, but a narrative about how all must leave behind their lives to answer the call to follow Christ. Each Christian is called to leave behind the life that was not centered in Christ; each believer lives and works in light of Jesus' call. Both partners follow Jesus, getting out of the boat as equals. It is this equality before God that becomes a foundation for a marriage or union that honors the gifts and faith of both. For both to live in covenant together as equals, each must see the working out of the other's faith as valid, just as important as his or her own. This is especially true for the one who is ordained—for while his or her faith is valued by the larger faith community, it is not always true for the other. No one enjoys second-rate status, especially in something so profound as faith. Whatever the baptismal ministries of both are, both are meant to be valued and equally explored.

For certain couples, the baptismal ministries of both partners lead to ordination. Their work and faith lives move along similar lines, even if they are not exactly the same. Like Priscilla and Aquila, these clergy couples may work together at the same craft. Some serve in the same church or ministry, others serve different faith communities. There is a common bond of ministry along with the bonds that bind them together in their personal lives. This can be a marvelous way to live in covenant relationship, but it is rarely a simple way. Issues of competition may arise within the relationship; there can be a lack of personal space—and the sense that the personal relationship and private life of the couple are extensions of their work in public ministry. The visions of ministry may be quite different from person to person, as may be work styles. It is important for each to hold the other's work and faith equal to his or her own, and to remember that there is more than one way to serve in ministry.

As noted earlier, one of the powerful messages of Aquila and Priscilla's work is that being Christian is not only about what is done as leaders of a worship community. How daily life is lived, what work is done, and how much compassion is shown outside the church walls bear witness to God as surely as the actions within the church. Paul, Priscilla, and Aquila valued their work as tentmakers, making that part of their relationship to God and to the world. The work done by ministers outside of their ministry is also important for revealing Christ's love to the world. This is easily forgotten when one or both partners pursue ordained ministry.

A simple example of this forgetting may be found in the cafeteria that provides meals for seminary students. Students take a break from their studies and their church work to enjoy a meal. There is usually a great deal of talking and listening to stories about various subjects and ideas while everyone gets meals, then everyone sits down. In the rush to get their meals and in their delight to see their friends, many seminarians forget to extend the most basic courtesy to those who prepare and serve their food. Some of them do not know the names of the people who serve them, even after years of seeing them daily. The lay work of those who serve and cook is not honored by those who will lead faith communities. These seminarians do not see their lives outside their ministry as crucial to how they live out their faith. There is a break between personal behavior and the call to ministry when one's life as a whole is not seen as integral to living out a baptismal ministry through ordained ministry.[15]

A lack of awareness about the way one's whole life reflects faith can also become an issue for the spouses and partners of ministers. Undervaluing activities that are not specifically "ministry" can lead to discounting much of daily life, sapping a great deal of meaning out of it. Priscilla and Aquila continued being tentmakers after becoming leaders of the faith community. The point is not to discount everything that is not clearly "ministry"; the point is to see the life of faith as something that is deepened and revealed in all that is and can be done. Whether it is mowing the lawn, shopping, preparing meals, or a hundred other tasks done every day, if it is done in good faith it will enrich the lives of all involved. Both partners need to value their own nonministry work as well as that of their spouses. The everyday tasks that must be done are also valuable and can lead to a deeper appreciation for the one who does them. Those tasks may also enrich the common life of both individuals in relationship.

Not all couples see their lives as united in their work and in their baptismal ministries. For many, their work lives are separate even while their marriage or union binds them together. There are spaces of separation in which each does his or her individual work. The story of Deborah and Lappidoth can provide a good biblical image for these couples, for while Deborah is identified by her marriage to Lappidoth, her calling to lead seems separate from her husband. There seems to be no partnership in work or ministry—or at least none that is elaborated upon.

For many, this may come closest to the reality of being a clergy spouse or partner. There are no specific guidelines on how to negotiate a public ministry and a private relationship. Lappidoth may or may not have assumed some of the duties that would usually fall to his wife, had she not been called to lead the tribes of Israel. His own work is not noted because it is not an integral part of Deborah's ministry. Lappidoth and Deborah did not leave behind a diary of how they lived out their marriage in light of her work, nor how Lappidoth's work was valued within the midst of that. In the gaps, there is room to imagine what a faithful and fruitful marriage might be in the context of Deborah's ministry. Did they share a common and deep faith? Did Lappidoth resent Deborah's extraordinary service as a political and religious leader? How can two remain equal before God and the community when only one is called to a professional ministry? There is a lot missing from their story, but what remains is that each is identified with the other. Deborah is not listed as separate from Lappidoth, but as his wife. Without Deborah, Lappidoth would not be identified at all. Keeping a mutual identification as a couple bound in covenant is the reality that most clergy spouses and partners live into; keeping that identification as one of two equals is what both must affirm and strengthen. This is as much the work of Deborah as it is Lappidoth, and as much Lappidoth's responsibility as it is Deborah's. That equality before God and in relationship may not be publicly acknowledged or affirmed, but it must be recognized and honored within the marriage or union.

Deborah and Lappidoth, and those in covenant relationships with ministers in this time, may live divergent lives when it comes to work. Each may live out faith in his or her own way, not necessarily sharing the same vision of faith or the same understanding of a common baptismal ministry. Perhaps there is no common faith that grounds the relationship, no mutual bond of baptism into the Christian faith and life. How will the common life of Deborah and Lappidoth look when they are not called to be united in a common vision of ministry, perhaps not even united in a common faith?

With the best of intentions for living in relationship together, some partners and spouses do not see themselves on a mutual journey of faith. Whether lay and ordained ministries are seen as equal is not the issue: there is no call and no wish to journey in faith together. This may be because there is no common faith, instead a union of two faiths. It may be that religious faith is not central to the identity and life of the clergy spouse or partner. In the end, there will be no stepping out in faith together. What happens at this point depends a great deal on the two involved, and how they understand their relationship. Can they agree to see their lives in fundamentally different ways while staying in covenant relationship? Do both understand their marriage as a sacred covenant, something that insures their equality and deepens their respect for the other? Faiths may be tested, sometimes found wanting. What are the possibilities for a clergy spouse or partner who does not want to take part in the call to ministry?

With a great deal of mutual care and respect, a couple could choose to live divergent but complementary lives. The call to ordained ministry is respected as a profession, but not as part of the spouse's fundamental context. Support for the ordained partner is present, but may not be grounded in a mutual context of baptismal ministry. Being a minister becomes much the same as any helping profession from the spouse's perspective. Little participation in ministry is expected by either partner. Whatever the partner pursues as his or her work will not necessarily be connected to a shared spiritual life. With a great deal of respect and humor, this may be a way to maintain a deep relationship with one following a call and the other staying in the boat. For couples who do not share the same religion or faith perspective, this provides a meeting place. The boundaries between personal life and professional call are exactly that: the difference between personal and professional life. The two do not meet; the couple avoids conflict by setting solid parameters. At the same time, this excludes working from a shared faith and baptismal identity. Whether that is possible depends on those involved. Leading divergent but complementary lives, separating the personal life from work, is one way of navigating the stormy waters of ministry.

Sometimes no common ground can be found, no agreement on how personal life and public ministry relate seems available. There may be no common ground of baptism, no shared faith, and no way to lead lives that complement each other. In this case, the one "called" leaves the partner behind in the boat, holding the nets and perhaps the remains of their former family life. The call to ministry is unacceptable to the partner, or the one called is unwilling or unable to let go of a particular vision of how the call is meant to be fulfilled. Rather than being bound in mutual respect in a covenant of union or marriage, one or both are unwilling or unable to be who they are if a call to ministry is accepted. If both are people of faith who once shared a common understanding, this can lead to a profound faith dilemma. If ordination is pursued and a call is taken in spite of the spouse's wishes, resentment builds. A lack of equal regard creeps in, often making life difficult. Perhaps a retreat into work and a hasty exit from shared life occurs.

For some the question arises: does a call to serve God make the relationship untenable? In other words, does God call people to ministry at the expense of their marriages and unions? If not, is it a matter of how the call is interpreted? Will the spouse be left behind in the boat for the good of God's work? If a call is answered, will the one who follows be tossed out of the boat?

TWO

The Other Half at Church

For most people who become ordained pastors and priests, ministry is located in a church. While some become hospital, prison, or campus chaplains, and still others work for nonprofit or political groups, most choose to serve a congregation. After completing the educational and denominational requirements comes the process of seeking a faith community. While most clergy and many of their partners have sought and found faith communities in the past, the search for a faith community postordination is remarkably different. For the clergyperson, the search is a job search as well as a quest for a faith community in which to serve God in Christ. The criteria and questions change in this process, and this change affects both partners in profound ways. What happens to the church experience of both when one searches for professional reasons while the other does not? What may once have been a "we" process, with both asking and looking for similar elements in a church, now becomes an "I" and "I" process, with two different lists of things to consider. There is a divergence of expectations, and a difference in the experience of the faith community. The starting point for this journey is the original list of questions that any couple may ask when seeking a faith community that will foster their baptismal ministries and help them serve Christ in the world.

PRE-ORDINATION/PROFESSIONAL CALL QUESTIONS: We-centered

There are many elements that come into play when seeking a faith community. Some are ones of convenience: how far away is the church? When are the worship services? Are the worship practices appealing? Then there are the deeper questions, ones that connect the personal faith lives of the couple with the ministry of a particular congregation: Do we feel God's presence here, with these people? Are our gifts needed and wanted? Does the worship here feed us spiritually? Can we see the love of Jesus Christ in these people? Is Jesus calling us to live our faith lives in communion with these people?

In the best of situations, the deep questions asked by both partners have the same answers. In many cases, one may feel a strong connection to a community while the other does not. This leads to further prayer and seeking if the couple cannot see themselves participating in the worship and service life of a particular church community. It takes time to find a community that can be a spiritual home for both partners.

In choosing a faith community, there is rarely a perfect fit. Individuals, couples, and communities have strengths and weaknesses. A deep relationship that is spiritually nurturing and allows for the baptismal ministries of all to flourish accepts shortcomings as an innate part of communal and covenantal life. If an individual or couple seeks perfection, there will never be a community of faith that will prove acceptable. Together, the couple must decide if a church can foster their growth as individuals and as a couple; just as important, the covenant partners must know that their gifts for ministry will be integral to the faith life of the community, fostering the faith lives of others while seeking to serve God in Christ's church. Profound joy and peace come with seeking to live in faith with others. The commitment to a community irrevocably shapes the faith journey of a couple, affecting the identity of both partners as individuals and as a covenant couple. Lives are changed, lived more fully for participating in the mission and worship of a church. This can lead to a greater connection between partners and spouses, for it touches upon the foundation of who they are in this world. When a church is sought and found by both partners, when joining a community is a decision made by both, then it becomes more than a search for individual spiritual depth. As with the marriage vows and promises, living in a particular faith community can deepen their connection. In other words, the "we" becomes the overarching reality of participation in church, nourishing both of the individuals while strengthening their commitment to one another and to God.

After years of professional training for ministry, the process of finding a faith community turns into something quite different. The questions that the ordained person asks become professional as well as personal. The questions of the spouse or partner also change, for his or her relationship with the faith community will be quite different from that of their call-seeking mates. What was once a difficult "we" list of questions branches into two separate "I" lists. At the outset, the "we" of community seeking is gone, replaced by the "I" and "I" agendas of the clergy and their spouses and partners. As their questions diverge, the possibilities for division increase.

ENTERING PROFESSIONAL MINISTRY: From a "We" Focus to "I and I" Reality

Because it is the clergyman or clergywoman who sets the parameters for seeking a faith community as a professional, the questions they bring to the search often take priority. Most must seek a faith community within their own denomination, often within a specific geographical area. Many are encouraged to seek a particular situation, often as an assisting pastor or the solo pastor of a small church. This narrows the choices in the search. Within the professional boundaries set before the man or woman seeking a call, the questions that each individual must ask of any particular congregation arise. The questions are personal and professional, for living out a baptismal ministry through full-time ordained ministry is most profoundly a personal claim of faith. It is in this personal relationship with God that the professional aspect finds its beginning.[1] One of the primary questions that each clergyperson must ask of any prospective faith community is whether a ministry in this specific church is something that is profoundly personal, faith-related, and professional. Is the call being considered only for professional reasons such as paid employment, geographical location, or status of the position? If the call is grounded in personal faith as well as professional interest, then several more critical questions arise:

- Do my gifts for leadership fit with this church's needs?
- Can I love these people, serve them, and foster their ministry in the world?

- Am I called to lead this community?
- Will my faith be enriched through serving in this place with these people?

These are difficult questions to ask, for they stretch beyond mere practicality and beyond mere emotional affection for a group of people. A minister could feel great affection for a particular community but realize that his or her gifts would not foster their ministry in the world. Perhaps the gifts for leadership fit well with the needs of a congregation but there is no personal connection. Unless taking a call will deepen the lives of all concerned, leading to a greater sense of God's presence and grace, the call is questionable. At times, the most pastoral thing to do is to decline a call, giving both the minister and the congregation the opportunity to continue seeking a more fruitful ministry partnership. This choice requires a lot of faith on the part of congregations and ministers because the search process for both is difficult. Ministers usually need to work to support themselves and churches need leaders, making it tempting to settle for a less than promising partner in ministry. The whole process is a leap of faith for all concerned, and that process is shared by clergy spouses and partners.

The partners and spouses of clergymen and clergywomen have a different set of questions that arises in this process. While they are not part of the professional aspect of the search process, the effects of the process for them are profound. Congregational search committees cannot consider the spouse or partner in their process because they are hiring a minister, not a team of a paid pastor and unpaid assistant pastor. At the same time, the happiness of the spouse or partner often determines whether a call is accepted and affects how long a pastor will remain. The spouse or partner does not set the parameters for seeking a faith community and cannot make a professional/personal choice for the other half. Often the concerns of the spouse go unsaid, making it difficult to address them openly. The questions that face the spouse or partner are separate from the ones of the ministers, but intimately related:

- Is God leading me here?
- Can I live in this context, with all that includes?

- Is this part of my faith journey, leading to a deeper connection with God?
- Is it possible for me to live out my own faith here?[2]
- Do I think my spouse/partner is called to serve this community?

None of these questions can be answered fully because it is impossible to see into the future and take into account all possible events and situations. At the same time, there should be a sense even at the outset that a particular situation holds the promise of fostering the faith lives of all involved. Life in covenant relationship is never easy. Adding professional concerns to the search for a faith community makes it even less so. But living out the baptismal calls of both may be immeasurably enriched through it all. When both partners are honest about their sense of call, and when the faith lives of both are recognized as equal before God, then the whole seeking process becomes a way of discerning the steps of faith for both. It is when one sacrifices his or her baptismal call to serve God that the whole thing becomes destructive.[3] A covenant relationship cannot survive unless mutual regard for the gifts of both involved remains. Disregard for the faith journey of either partner leads to spiritual resentment and bankruptcy that can shatter marriages and unions.

A CALL ACCEPTED: The "I and I" Reality Reigns

After a specific call is accepted, for better and for worse, the whole experience of faith community changes for both covenant partners. The faith community was chosen with prayerful consideration for both professional and personal reasons. In the best of situations, the needs of both covenant partners were considered before the call was accepted. From this point on, the experience of being in a faith community will not be a shared one. Even if both partners remain in the same worship community, how they are and who they are within that community is no longer held in common.

The first and most profound change that separates the experience of the spouse or partner from that of the full-time professional minister half is the relationship with the congregation. The one serving as pastor is the professional, while the spouse or partner is not. The spouse or partner was not chosen by the community, while the minister was. The congregation knows how to relate to a pastor, but may not know how to address the spouse or partner. How well he or she is welcomed into the community—if he or she decides to become part of it—often has more to do with the spouse or partner of the previous pastor than with the incoming one. What are the expectations involved? While the expectations of the pastor have been reviewed for professional reasons, there are usually nonprofessional expectations that meet the new spouse or partner at the church door. How flexibly these are held can indicate the congregation's ability to see the spouse or partner as an individual rather than as a mobile, detached appendage of the pastor. No one wants to be thought of as a third arm.

The covenant partners are no longer on equal footing within the faith community. One is a professional, the other not. One has been asked to lead the church in serving Christ in the world. The other may or may not be involved. The minister is a professional religious person, whom many credit with a great spiritual depth. The spouse or partner is an unknown entity. The pastor is considered a person in his or her own right; the partner is sometimes seen as an extension. Even if the faith community is willing and able to foster the faith lives of both, the roles have changed. Being a minister is a public role, being a spouse a semiprivate one. Everyone knows who the partner is, but what is the place for him or her?

For some, moving from choosing a faith community as equals, the preordination "we" reality, means taking on a title: clergy spouse, or clergy partner. The relationship is no longer private, but has become a role within the community. What that role is might vary from church to church, time to time, and culture to culture, but the fact that there is a role remains. The clergy partner may be expected to fill various roles within the church itself. The clergy spouse may find his or her actions scrutinized in ways that the actions of others are not. The clergy partner may enhance or weaken the ministry of his or her clergy half by conforming or not conforming to a set of unstated but powerful expectations. Whether these expectations reside firmly within the community, are a product of the partner's own experiences, or the interplay of both may change from situation to situation. What remains is the feeling that there are personal and public issues involved that were not there before ordination became part of the covenant reality.

When a call to ordained ministry is the way one partner works out his or her baptismal ministry, the baptismal ministry of the nonordained partner must be worked out within a context set by career ministry reality. Whether a spouse or partner chooses to work out a lay baptismal ministry in the same faith community or in a different one, the very choice is a result of the call to ordination. The overall context is set by the professional calling. There is no option to work out both baptismal ministries in a fostering community without the differentiating reality of ordination. In most cases, the faith community that fostered the couple in the beginning is left behind. Usually, a change of location is involved, making it difficult if not impossible for the spouse or partner to remain in the original faith community. If the couple remains in the original faith community, which occurs in some traditions more than others, there is still a new relationship that must grow. There is no way to return to a pre-ordination reality, whether remaining in the original church or serving a new community. A new reality has grown out of the whole ordination process and it costs the covenant couple their former relationships with fostering faith communities.

If the couple does not share the same faith, or if the spouse or partner understands ministry as a helping profession rather than a faith-rooted calling, the changes still occur. Perhaps two faith communities are left. When a move is involved, the couple loses everyday contact with friends and family. An entire web of support and care changes from daily reality to an occasional long distance visit. No matter how good communication is, there is a marked difference between local and long distance relationships. Being with friends and family on a regular basis cannot be replaced by phone calls, e-mails, and visits. This is a very real part of relocation and it is a loss to both partners in covenant relationship. The difference is that the ordained partner's choice governs the loss of the old context and the selection of the new. With great hope and faith they drive off to the new community; with sadness they both mourn the loss of the community in the rearview mirror.

THE NEW REALITY SETS IN

Once a call to serve a church is taken, the minister in the relationship is committed to a particular community. For the spouse or partner, a choice must be made. Should he or she participate in the community of call or seek another faith community? If a common faith is not part of the marriage, this has already been decided. The spouse or partner seeks his or her own congregation and continues a separate life of faith. If a common faith exists, then the decision of where to go on Sunday remains. It is a decision that has profound implications for the daily life of both partners in covenant relationship. There are consequences to both staying together in a community and to living out the faith in separate churches.

Choosing to Stay

One of the first things that must be discerned is how much can be said to those within the faith community. There are conversations that a spouse or partner does not have because they may harm the relationship between the minister and the community. A judicious silence is kept about negative feelings. If a spouse or partner is angry or annoyed with something, he or she does not share that with the people at church. Criticism can be perceived as petty or can be taken as a sign that the minister is gravely flawed in ways that prohibit his or her service to the church. No one thinks twice if someone complains about the dirty socks left on the floor every day. But what if it's the minister who is leaving them around? Does that mean that he or she has dangerous character flaws running much deeper than laundry? Obviously, there are more important issues that cause anger and annoyance than a disregard for laundry, but a casual remark can be taken with unreasonable seriousness.

No one is perfect, but many expect that a pastor is a bit closer to perfection than everyone else. Any sign that he or she has the same clay feet as the rest of humanity, with or without casting off socks, may be troubling for individuals within the church. This does not mean that any minister or clergy partner should try to be perfect, or try to seem perfect. What it does mean is that admissions of imperfection are easier to accept coming from the source rather than a spouse or partner. For instance, if the pastor is less than organized at home or at work, disclosing that is not the place of his or her partner.

There are conversations that clergy spouses and partners do not have with members of their partner's faith community. If a partner questions ministry choices in leading the faith community, often silence is maintained. No matter how understanding a congregant might be, there are conversations that cross a line, reflecting on the pastor's abilities and character. The clergyperson must be able to serve and lead the faith community. Too much information about his or her personal life may take away the ability to do that. For that reason, the partner often remains silent on personal issues. To confide in those within the church about personal issues can damage relationships. To remain silent, if there are no outside people in whom to confide, can harm the covenant relationship. It is not easy to maintain a respectful silence in matters great and small, but it is usually necessary.

If a partner maintains a judicious silence in matters that might damage the relationship between the congregation and the pastor, the same cannot be said of the members of the congregation. Personal stories are told to the spouses and partners of clergy, sometimes ill timed and in unwanted numbers. The spouse often hears confessions without warning, at coffee hour after worship, in the grocery check-out line, during choir practice, and in many other contexts. Perhaps it is because the congregants feel that the spouse is the next best thing to the pastor. Perhaps it is a way to communicate with the minister indirectly. Whatever the reason, the partner becomes an extension of the pastor, a convenient link. This "confessions-r-us" situation is difficult and usually not something the partner or spouse encourages. It is a messy and sometimes embarrassing business, and it is often difficult to respond to it. Should a spouse shut down the confession and gently suggest a direct discussion with the minister? How can a partner make the one revealing his or her life situation aware that such a confession ought to be made in a private therapy session or isolated in an office?

Sometimes members of the faith community assume that a spouse knows details of conversations they have had with the pastor. Revelations are made to the partner with the assumption that the background is already known. It becomes difficult for the spouse or partner to know so many private things about so many people because many of those things are painful. They are not easy to forget and they color future relationships with those in the church.

Every faith community has its share of disagreements and meetings in which members behave badly. It is a community for imperfect humans. Ugly things happen. The spouse or partner of the minister sees the ugliness in the faith community because of his or her covenant relationship. Anger and pettiness may not govern the community's work, but it is a constant in every community to a greater or lesser degree. The partner often gets a front row seat for it all. The illusion of perfect harmony and good will doesn't last very long for a clergy spouse. For better and for worse, the church community is revealed, in all its wonder and all its pettiness. There are no rose-colored glasses that can hide the truth.

For many spouses and partners, remaining in the same worship community as their clergy counterparts means losing an individual faith identity. They are not seen as independent believers coming into the community, but as the partners of the leaders. This is simply the truth of the situation, but it can lead to the partner being seen as an extension of the minister—a helpful one, perhaps, but still an extension. Some feel like they are mere shadows, drawing their outline from their other half, with little or no substance of their own. If they participate in the ministries of the church, then it's just what is expected of them. Their gifts may not be seen as a way to live out their own baptismal ministry, but as the way to live out the ordained ministry of their partner. If the spouse or partner begins to see himself or herself as an extension, then something precious is lost: the profound truth that before God the working out of baptismal ministry is a holy and blessed endeavor. No one should ever be made to feel like the shadow of another, especially in faith.

Friendships within the faith community have a built-in inequality for clergy spouses and partners. Many in the church feel that they have to be on their best church behavior around the clergy family. It is difficult to form friendships when everyone involved is careful to screen out the parts of them that make them who they really are. Friends are honest about themselves and accepted for who they are. A lack of honesty and openness may lead to pleasant conversation and activities of mutual interest, but it won't lead to a friendship that will last. This is a great loss to spouses and partners because sharing faith can enrich friendships and provide companions on the marvelous journey of faith.

Another loss for the spouse or partner is being alone in the pew every Sunday. The two no longer sit side by side. They do not experience worship in the same way. The "we" that use to be together in worship is now two "I's" that are separated by the tasks of ministry. The solidarity that comes of common worship is broken. It may be replaced by a solidarity rooted in the mutual affirmation of each partner's faith life, but it may not. This is a separation that cannot be changed, and it will have a profound effect on both.[4]

For the partner sitting in the pew, the experience of worship is never what it was before the ordination and a church profession. The sermon is heard in a different way because it comes from someone inside the family. The worship experience becomes something that is no longer from an outside source. If no one can be a prophet in his or her own town, then no one can be a prophet to his or her spouse. How a partner hears a sermon or participates in the life of the church community changes. An outside resource for deepening faith and exploring baptismal ministry has morphed into an in-house affair. No longer is the perspective of the pastor taken in the same way. The message and the messenger are too closely related for many spouses and partners.

When a partner chooses to remain in the same faith community, he or she is still not worshiping with the covenant partner. The spouse or partner often arrives at a different time. The two do not sit together in worship. Any weekly social gatherings are work situations for one, robbing both of shared personal experiences in the community. The focus for the covenant couple is no longer the same. They are no longer sharing their worship experiences directly: they are just having them simultaneously and in the same geographical area.

For the average person in the pew, attending church is something that nourishes. Community members gather to be fed spiritually. Pastors and other leaders are working to pull the spiritual banquet together, serving and hosting. That is a different experience of worship, one that can be equally enriching while remaining a separate experience. In this metaphor of serving and being served, where is the spouse or partner? He or she is not working, but does not share the experience of the other members of the community. Rather than enjoying the banquet as a beloved guest or as a servant, the partner can be removed from the experience. Unable to enjoy either role fully, the partner or spouse is often doing the equivalent of eating over the sink before the event! He or she may have the same elements that the others share in worship, but the experience is not shared on a deep level. Worship services are gotten through rather than lived into. The communion of bread and wine that binds together those participating may not bring a sense of the holy or a sense of community for a spouse or partner. What can result is a loneliness all the more profound because it is felt in the midst of those who find themselves brought together in communion with God and each other. If a partner's experience of church becomes one of isolation rather than communion, his or her spiritual life will be damaged. A break from the community may be the only way to continue living a deep faith life.

Choosing Another Church

There are many reasons for a partner or spouse to choose a faith community that is separate from his or her clergy partner's work. For some, participating in a different community is not a personal loss because the worship experience within the clergy partner's community was not a shared one. Given that, the difference is one of geography. Not able to worship fully together, choosing a different community becomes the way the two in covenant worship as individuals. With this split, the working out of their covenant vows to one another is removed from their experience of a faith community. There are positives and negatives to this situation. The call to ordination now separates the two in their community experiences in a physical way. There is no common community, even with differing roles. There are now two faith communities in play rather than one, making it more difficult to negotiate how the baptismal ministries of both will be worked out in some common way.

With a decision to join a separate faith community, the spouse or partner is no longer the clergy spouse or clergy partner at church. The baptismal ministry is not seen in light of the ordained ministry of his or her partner. There are no role expectations other than that of congregant. A certain anonymity returns, making it possible for the partner to be his or her own person of faith. For some, this is the only way to live a life of faith as more than an appendage of a partner's professional ministry. The freedom to be an individual in one's own right returns.

When a clergy spouse decides to choose a separate faith community, there are more possibilities than if he or she stays at the church of call. The choice is no longer limited by denominational affiliation or ministry requirements. The partner can choose a community based upon the congregation rather than its denomination. This is especially appealing if he or she comes from a different denomination than his or her clergy half.

With a move to another community, the partner gets to have a pastor, someone to seek with questions and doubts. Someone outside the family is available as a chaplain in times of illness or crisis. This is a gift to the ordained partner as well. He or she is relieved of pastoral duties when his or her own family is in need. In those times, the covenant partners can let go of pastoral duties and focus on being family, letting someone else bring a gracious ministering presence into their lives. In times of crisis, both covenant partners need to be with one another not as pastor and layperson, but as two bound together by love and held in God's love. When a spouse chooses another faith community, a pastor outside their union can be their minister. This is a marvelous gift to them both.

It is clear that many clergy spouses and partners choose to live out their baptismal ministries, or their own distinct faith, apart from the congregation of their ordained partners. This can lead to separate but complementary faith lives. Both live out their ministries while remaining committed to one another. Rather than support an ordained ministry by being present and participating, the partner supports the ordained partner, sending him or her off to ministry with blessings. There is support for the person in ministry, but not a sharing of that ministry's location. The ordained partner supports the choice of his or her spouse by showing deep respect and support for the lay work done in the chosen congregation.[5]

When the couple decides to live out their faith lives in separate communities, there may be ramifications for the ordained spouse. If there are expectations of the clergy spouse, then an absent spouse will challenge them. If the clergy partner role is well established in the community, whatever its contents may be, then an absent partner may be disappointing. When the partner is not a member of the community of call, some within that community may see it as a personal slight or outright rejection. If this creates tension, then it may be necessary to address the issue directly. This is a task for the minister, for it is his or her community of call.[6]

Choosing to participate in separate communities may make it more difficult for the couple to connect their individual faith lives. It is easy for both to divorce their ongoing faith journeys from those of their other half. This is understandable, for keeping track of two communities and how they enrich faith (or make it more difficult to be faithful!) is not easy. The sermons heard and preached are different. The educational offerings are unrelated. The physical location is different. These elements can make for deep and prayerful conversations between the partners because they provide another view of how the Christian faith is working in the world. With a great deal of time, effort, and understanding, the two separate communities will bring to the covenant relationship a depth that can be a profound blessing. But these very complexities, the serious nature of the elements involved, can serve as an excuse not to relate the two faith journeys. The amount of time and energy it takes to have the prayerful conversations is significant. If that time cannot be found, or both partners are not willing to devote such time and energy to keeping their faith journeys in close relationship, then their faith journeys diverge. These journeys can be complementary if disconnected, but more likely they are not. There is a real possibility that the two become strangers in their faith lives, leaving that aspect of their living unrelated. This can be a profound loss for both, a loss not foreseen when they entered into their covenant marriage or union.

Whether the couple decides to remain in the same community or go their separate ways on Sunday, living in light of ordained ministry is difficult. What happens when problems arise? Who will be the pastor for the couple?

WHOM DO YOU SEEK?

In time of spiritual need, most people within a faith community seek out their pastor. He or she is a resource for individuals and couples when spiritual questions arise, when marriage is planned, and when children arrive. If there are difficulties in a relationship, the pastor can refer couples and individuals to a therapist or a group that may help. He or she is a resource in times of crisis. But what about the pastor and the pastor's partner? Who will be their pastoral resource?

In most towns, there are several churches led by several different ministers. The obvious choice may be to seek a local minister when guidance is needed. Unfortunately, this is not always a step that can be taken with confidence. The local ministers are in many ways coworkers for the ordained half of the couple. They may serve on the same boards, work together in joint ministries, and be part of the same clergy support group. They may be part of the same ministerium, a group of clergy who work in close proximity.

There is a professional relationship that may make the local ministers a poor choice for the covenant couple. Questions arise. Will this minister keep confidential the discussions of the couple? Will seeking help locally have professional repercussions? Will the views of the ordained person be taken more seriously than those of the spouse? Can this minister be objective enough to help the couple, providing a safe place for them to discuss their relationship to one another and their ongoing spiritual paths to serve God? Sometimes, but not always, dodging the local ministers and seeking help outside of the area is the only way that the couple can get the help needed.

When a local minister is not an option, then someone else must be found. In most areas, there are therapists and spiritual advisors who are not involved with the same religious community. Driving to another town to find a therapist or chaplain can give the couple an outside resource that does not affect the professional work of the ordained partner. It can also give the lay partner a resource person who assumes that the views of both are equally important.

Within some denominations, resources are made available to clergy and family members. The leaders of presbyteries, dioceses, conferences, and associations are aware of the toll that ordained ministry exacts from couples and provide lists of therapists and counselors to serve as resources in times of need. In an effort to support the clergy who serve their churches, these overarching structures can be a good resource. If the pressures associated with full-time ministry corrode the covenant relationships of the clergy, then the clergy will not last long as congregational leaders. If there are no resources for the clergy and his or her partner, then a choice between remaining married or remaining in ordained ministry can become a sad reality. It is in the best interest of all to provide support for spouses and clergy before it comes to such a choice.

When a couple find the pastoral and therapeutic support needed to sustain their relationship with each other, when the spiritual growth of both is fostered within their relationship and by outside sources, the couple has a much better chance of maintaining a growing and rewarding union. This does not mean that there will be no more tension, or that issues involving ministry and personal life will be miraculously solved. It does mean that the hard work and mutual affection of both will create a sustainable and nourishing bond that cannot only survive ordained ministry but can become deeper because of it. There is a grace about living into baptismal ministries, and those that lead to ordination, that is a gift of God.

Beyond the needs for keeping a marriage or union strong, there are also social needs. Both the ordained spouse and the nonordained partner need other people in their lives. Friendship is vital but often difficult to maintain for the clergy couple. For this reason, some join support groups for clergy and spouses. While some of these are based on a therapeutic model, many are just gatherings to provide friendship and conversation. There is something wonderful about conversing with others who share the same joys and problems of life in light of ordination. Clergy and spouses don't have to edit their language or talk only about religious issues. There are no confessions about lack of church attendance or discussion about intentions to return to church soon. These groups can provide a place for relaxation and conversation without the need to take up the roles of clergy and partner. Sharing with others in similar circumstances can be a wonderful gift to a couple.

Another important resource for spouses and partners of clergy are friends outside the church community. Finding friends can be difficult for both the ordained and nonordained halves because so much time and energy goes into the faith community. Because clergy families may not stay in one community for more than a few years, friendships become long distance almost as quickly as they are made. There is very little continuity in friendships for the couple; even if friendships are maintained after relocation, they are not local. Spending time with friends in person is vital and life-enhancing. Without friends in the community, the lives of clergy and partners are lacking one of the greatest joys of being human.

Many covenant partners make friends with others while in seminary. The common experiences they share can create a bond that sustains them as individuals and as a couple. The seminary or divinity school experience provides a group of people who know one another before setting out to serve in an ordained ministry. Those who prepare for ministry, and the spouses who support them, understand that ministers are not perfect. They can provide a great reality check for each other, reminding one another that all stand equal before God. They can also listen to one another, be discussion partners for one another, and accept one another as friends. These friendships can survive distance, life changes, and any circumstance that ministry brings about. They take time to develop and they take great care to continue. They are worth every effort.

There is one crucial element in the lives of clergy spouses and partners that is rarely addressed: the need for a spiritual guide not only in times of stress and anxiety, but in the ordinary times. The gifts and needs of the ordained partner are usually acknowledged because they are critical to professional development and effectiveness. This is not true of the spouses' gifts and the partners' needs. When the equality of the two living in covenant is recognized, then the spiritual life of the nonordained partner must be considered as important as that of his or her clergy partner. Spiritual discernment is not a gift for ordained people only, but a gift that should be available to all members of the faith. A spiritual director or a fostering spirituality group can provide the context that values the inner life of a spouse not because he or she is a spouse, but because he or she is a person of faith who left behind boat and net to follow Jesus. Ignatian spiritual practices, monthly spiritual direction, or planned retreats remind both the clergy and the partner that they are equal before God and in following Christ. In working out their baptismal ministries, both fulfill their inner callings as equals, regardless of how those callings appear to the outside world. Partners should seek spiritual guidance and care in the best and the worst of times. This may or may not be made easier by denominational affiliations, but is worth seeking regardless.

HONORING A DAY OF REST AND RECONNECTION

Many pursue ordination because of a deeply held faith and a profound appreciation for Sabbath. The postordination irony is that such a day of rest and reconnection with God and others is difficult to observe. The same is true for the partners and spouses of those ordained. What happens to the spiritual lives of spouses when Sunday becomes a workday for their other halves? When the faith community becomes a workplace rather than a place of worship and rest only, what happens to Sabbath?

Sabbath is not merely a two-hour time slot that the church services and coffee hours fill. *Sabbath* is the day given over to God and one another. It is a time to connect with God in Christ through worship. It is the time set aside to delight in others rather than interact with them for business or mutual interest. It is a time set aside to remind all the faithful that all time belongs to God, and that all time is sacred when dedicated to God. It is not a time of deprivation, but a time to come face to face with God in Christ. Sabbath reminds the worshiping faithful that they are God's creatures, made in the divine image and loved fully at all times. On a day of Sabbath rest, all the faithful have the opportunity to remember their sacred identities, and to see in others the face of Christ. Sabbath is the gift of true sight and the inbreaking of peace into the ordinary weeks of human life. Without this time set aside, it is too easy to forget the sanctity of others, the uniqueness of each individual, and the presence of God in the world. It is not a time of checking out of the world, but a time for seeing the world and human life as it truly is. For the faithful, it is a time of rejuvenation, a renewal of faith that sustains, and the opportunity to seek the face of Christ in the world of everyday living. But if Sunday is a workday, when is the Sabbath for the pastor's partner? When is the Sabbath rest for the ordained? When does the covenant couple come before God for nourishment and rest?

BEING SINGLE EVERY SUNDAY

One of the most difficult realities that comes with a congregational ministry is the separation the couple encounters every Sunday. While most couples whose lives do not involve ordained ministry go their separate ways for work, clergy and partners must separate for worship—a weekly communal event that could be shared in previous years. For the spouse, this means being single every Sunday.[7] The partner often arrives for worship or Christian education alone. If there happens to be more than one worship service every Sunday, then arriving and leaving the worship community are separate activities for the couple. The partner sits without his or her other half throughout the worship service. This often holds true for any adult educational offerings. This separation extends even into the Sunday social gatherings such as weekly coffee hours. While the couple may be in the same room, perhaps even in the same conversation group, they are still separated by the duties of ministry. For the minister, coffee hour, worship, and adult education gatherings are work events. They may be rewarding and nourishing, but they are never merely social.

If the couple has children, the feeling of being single every Sunday is intensified. Not only is there no common experience of worship, there is no one to help with the children. There is no sharing of parental duties, allowing each to enjoy time in worship or at other community events. If a child is sick, it is never the minister who stays home on Sunday, missing vital prayer, education, and worship time. The partner is a single parent every Sunday, responsible for the total care of the children.[8] A spouse may be physically present in worship, whether in the same community or a different one, and be so busy tending children that the experience of worship is lost. Rather than participating in a life-giving service of worship, the partner is struggling to survive to the end of it. This is not true every week, for there are good and trying experiences for all parents who raise their children in the faith community, but it is true some weeks. The worship time of the spouse or partner trying to live out his or her baptismal ministry is no longer guaranteed. It is contingent upon the children's health and ability to sit in church. Something wonderful is gained when children are present in church, for the parents as well as the whole congregation. At the same time, the time of silence, of collecting oneself and preparing for worship, disappears. Between insuring the child's happiness and keeping up with the worship service, that precious time of individual focus and prayer is lost. These things can be addressed with child care and the help of others, but there is no replacing the partner who is no longer side by side in the pew, sharing in the work and the worship.

For some, these elements of being single on Sunday create a spiritual straightjacket—something that binds and prevents any freedom of movement for the spirit. The partner may know that he or she is surrounded by a whole community of people gathered to come into God's presence, but may not feel part of it. In the midst of communal worship, the spouse may feel alone. This can be a terrible drain upon his or her spiritual life, leaving an exhaustion of the soul that is difficult to overcome. The spouse got out of the boat to follow Jesus but suddenly feels as if he or she is back in the boat. This time, the boat is surrounded by seawater, something that is overwhelming and cannot refresh the wilting spirit. How is it possible that honoring the calling of a covenant partner to ordained ministry can lead to such a desolate place?

SURROUNDED BY HOLINESS, HELD IN GOD'S LOVE

What can be done when worship is no longer what it once was? Where is the grace in being alone in a pew every Sunday, either in the same building as the clergy half, or in a different one? Where are peace and a time to be with God when there is no one to help tend the children during worship? What happened to the mutual journey of faith?

These questions arise and there are no simple answers to them. Life after ordination will never be the same as life before it. There are things that are lost that will not return as long as one sits in the pew while the other stands in front of the congregation. For many spouses and partners, it takes a great leap of faith to find new ways to nourish the spirit and find a place in a community of faith. Each person must chart a new course because ordination pushes everyone into new and often rough waters. While the clergy half may find help readily available through his or her professional training and resources, the partner may not be so lucky. But there is great hope and great adventure in charting a new course, especially when help is offered. Rough waters do not have to be navigated alone, nor without a map.

> Why must I walk about mournfully
> because of the oppression of the enemy?
> O send your light and your truth;
> let them lead me;
> let them bring me to your holy hill
> and to your dwelling.
> Then I will go to the altar of God,
> to God my exceeding joy;
> and I will praise you with the harp,
> O God, my God. (Psalm 43:2b–4)

When worship that was such a vital part of faith withers, it is time to cry out to God. While there is rarely an enemy out to destroy a spouse or partner, it can feel like an assault on faith when the experience of worship is no longer shared or even guaranteed to be available. There is a relief in mourning the loss of shared worship and the loss of the worship experience due to child-care duties. This mourning is not something to wallow in, but it is a vital part of moving into the new reality and getting one's bearings in a new ocean of faith experience.

Living into a new way of experiencing worship can be like being pulled out to sea in a rowboat. The circumstances are too overwhelming to fight with the pathetic oars provided. The only way to survive is to let the tide lead to unknown places. On the old nautical maps, unknown spots were labeled, "Here Be Dragons." The familiar shore of pre-ordination worship disappears and the new shore is nowhere in sight. Such a trip changes everything, for there is no going back to the old ways. While dragons may not appear, the knowledge that there is a whole world beyond the small, comfortable shore will reframe worship forever—whether that worship is in the same community or elsewhere. The trip, though difficult, can also be a blessing.

In the Psalms are words that give voice to this loss and also bring hope for a new way of living a blessed faithful life. These songs are prayers to God, giving the pray-er the words needed to express deep sadness and loss. At the same time, they are faithful conversations with God, for there is always the assurance that God is listening.

> Be merciful to me, O God, be merciful to me,
> for in you my soul takes refuge;
> in the shadow of your wings I will take refuge,
> until the destroying storms pass by.
> I cry to God Most High,
> to God who fulfills his purpose for me. (Psalm 57:1–2)

At times when the experience of faith seems absent, when the separation of clergy and spouse seems to lead only to disappointing worship, it is comforting to know that the lives of both have a God-given purpose that will be fulfilled. Living into that fulfillment will be different in postordination reality, but it is present and a path will be found. Spouses and partners should cry out in pain and frustration, shouting out their feelings to God. All are held in God's holiness, even when circumstances conspire to hide this truth. In faith, the destroying storms will pass. The pre-ordination life has been swept away by these storms, but a new life comes in its wake. Living into that new life is difficult but full of hope.

THREE

The Second Career?

> I am a serious career woman whose career has been adapted to fit my husband's call to ministry. When I relocate, I have to explain that my short tenure in previous positions was not due to my lack of ability, but to my husband's relocations for ministry.

> My spouse says my work is important, but it doesn't always feel as if it's treated as important. The primary reason I work freelance is so that I can make my schedule flex around my spouse's. What corporate America job will let me have a Sunday through Thursday workweek? . . . The fact that it's almost always me who ends up rearranging a work schedule and sacrificing work time makes me feel as if my job is of lesser importance.[1]

The primary focus of this chapter is not financial necessity or gain, but how the career of the spouse or partner is affected by the clergy half. As a way to begin this exploration, an overall picture of how work and money relate in a clergy and spouse relationship is a good place to start.

In 1994, Michael Lane Morris and Priscilla White Blanton studied clergy marriages to see what work-related problems they faced and how those pressures compared to the marriages of nonministry couples. In "The Influence of Work-Related Stressors on Clergy Husbands and Their Wives," they found that "95% of all clergy are grossly underpaid, given their educational level. Clergy rank in the top 10% of the population in terms of education, but rank 325th out of 432 occupations in terms of salary."[2] These figures were based upon a pool of respondents, of whom "80% served as a senior pastor in their parish, working a mean of 51 hours per week in ministerial responsibilities in parishes averaging 300–500 members. They had been in the ministry approximately 17 years, had been at their current parish for a mean of 8 years, and had moved three or four times since entering the ministry. Interestingly, 14% indicated that they needed to work either part- or full-time in other areas to assist the family in meeting financial obligations."[3] The respondents to this study were not fresh out of seminary, starting at the bottom of the salary and compensation ladder. These were men (no women ministers were included, perhaps because they were relatively rare in the 1980s) in their prime earning years, working in larger-than-average churches, and working more than fifty hours a week at their positions. Yet, 95 percent were grossly underpaid in comparison to those in other professions who had equivalent educations. Forty-four percent of the ministers who participated in this study lived in parsonages, manses, or rectories—houses owned by the churches that employed them.[4] While living in church-owned homes, the clergy family builds up no equity, which can have grave financial consequences for their retirement years.

Although the focus of this study was the clergy career rather than that of the spouses, the importance of the spouse's career was noted. The wives of these ministers were relatively well educated, with more than one-third holding bachelor's degrees, and 18 percent holding graduate degrees.[5] Seventy-six percent of these clergy wives worked outside the home."[6] This is not surprising when seen in light of their husbands' compensation: many of the couples may have needed the second income for living expenses. Necessity can govern whether a spouse or partner works and the amount of time spent working because the second income may make the ordained ministry financially possible. It is not the only reason a partner or spouse may choose to work, but it is an important part of the overall situation. Spouses and partners may work to fulfill their own call to live in faith. Having the opportunity do work that is meaningful is a gift, and one that may be part of the baptismal calling.

The choice of a career in ordained ministry affects the overall quality of the covenant relationship. It is not only a financial element, not merely a means to personal fulfillment, but something that affects a couple's overall quality of life. In their study of clergy and their wives, Morris and Blanton noted that the intrusions into family life that came from ordained ministry affected the satisfaction of both the husband and the wife.[7] The more intrusive the ministry became, the less satisfied the couple were in their married life. The same was true in relation to the satisfaction levels of parenting—the more intrusive the ministry, the less satisfaction both felt in their roles as parents.[8] It is in their roles as parents that a significant difference arises. It is this difference that is profoundly affected by the work of the spouse.

Morris and Blanton note that while the husbands' parental satisfaction could be predicted by the amount of work intrusion, for the wives a second factor arose. In parental satisfaction, time demands were a critical factor. They write,

> For wives, time demands also influenced parental satisfaction. No doubt the time demands many spouses of clergy encounter are the result of absorptive role demands endemic to the clergy profession (Kieran & Munro, 1988). The clergy profession could be considered what Papanek (1973) called a "two-person career," which assumes that the wife's role is an integral part of the husband's occupational role, and usually goes unpaid, unrecognized, and unappreciated (Thompson & Walker, 1989; Voydanoff, 1987). For many spouses of clergy, the role is extremely complex, as they are often expected to serve as unpaid assistant pastors. Thus, many spouses perform three full-time occupations (e.g. family, church, personal career) and are remunerated for one.[9]

For some spouses, the ordained ministry of their other half leads to a shortage of time. If the clergy half is underpaid, then the spouse or partner may have to work a significant number of hours each week to support the family. The demands of the ordained ministry may mean that the work of family life falls to the nonordained spouse. If there are expectations that the partner or spouse will also work in the faith community, then what happens to the spouse's schedule? There isn't enough time to do everything, but the partner may not feel free to opt out of one of these three areas of work. Without the willingness or ability to drop one of the three occupations (family, church, personal career), the spouse is always busy, always overbooked, and always struggling under a mountain of unfinished work. There is no time to focus on just one or two of the occupations, leading to dissatisfaction with all three. Each of the occupations is done at the expense of another. Struggling to do all three jobs takes a heavy toll on the body, mind, and spirit of the clergy spouse. Getting through the day with all family members intact becomes the goal rather than enjoying family life. His or her covenant relationship suffers as other demands remove the time and energy needed to foster its growth. Parenting, which takes a great amount of time and energy, becomes a source of guilt and exhaustion rather than joy. A career that should be fulfilling work becomes a burden rather than a means for serving the world and growing as a person. For those not interested in a career outside of home and church, a paying job becomes a necessity that takes away valuable time and energy without enriching the life of the individual or family. Financial survival and fulfilling family and ministry expectations rob the partner of joy and may leave him or her wondering why the call to ordained ministry has turned into a constant source of frustration. How can this situation be transformed into something life-giving for the spouse or partner?

WORK IS MORE THAN A SUPPLEMENTAL PAYCHECK

The work of the spouse or partner, whether a career intentionally followed or a means to financial gain, is a way to serve the world as an individual. A job done well, with consideration for others and intentional care, gives something back to the community. Getting a paycheck and accomplishing goals are valuable to the world and to the working person. In a world that often judges personal worth by work and wages, a career can enhance the self-perception of a spouse or partner. Contributing to the finances of the family may bring with it a stronger sense of equality within the covenant relationship, and a greater say in the financial decisions made for the family.[10]

Whether a spouse or partner works by choice or necessity, the work and the time spent doing it deserve respect. The work of the spouse, whether it be waiting tables in a local restaurant or serving as the local pediatrician, is not an extension of the other half's ordained ministry. A spouse's work is his or her own, not only a means to a supplemental paycheck that requires no thought or regard by the ministering half. The work of any person is valuable in its own right, not merely as something that makes another person's career and calling possible. A partner should be supported by the clergy half, just as the ordained minister is supported by the nonordained partner. To devalue lay work, done as a meaningful career or as a means to support family life, is to hold the partner's time less valuable. There must be equal regard for the career efforts of both, helping to maintain and foster a sense of equality and care within the covenant relationship.

A career that is separate from the ordained ministry of the clergy half gives the spouse or partner a way to be in the world that is independent of ministry. At work it is not the clergy half who is the main focus: the clergy is the supporting spouse. This can bring a greater sense of worth and equality into the marriage or union.

The workplace of the partner or spouse can also be a place of support. Friendships can be formed without fear of repercussions within the faith community. Through work, the couple may find friends that do not expect pastoral care or saintly behavior.

WORKING OUT BAPTISMAL MINISTRY THROUGH MEANINGFUL WORK

What am I called to do in this world? How should my gifts be used for the good of all? How do I serve God and my neighbor? The gifts for serving Christ in the world find their expression through meaningful work, whether that work is recognized as a ministry or not. Just as an ordained ministry is the way for the clergy half to live out a baptismal call to serve God and the world, secular work may be the holy calling of the partner. One is not intrinsically more valuable than the other because both are ways to live faithfully. Whether this is recognized by the world at large, or even by a particular church community, is not of primary importance. Faithful discernment of call, lay or ordained, leads to true service and to a working out of God's grace in this world. No one's work should be devalued because it is not a ministry in the obvious sense. In this complex world, grace enters through many doors. The work of a partner or spouse may well bring God's peace to bear upon the world. It may not be easily recognized, but it is still precious.

The value of a person's work is seen in many professions, including one that many people give little thought to: the school bus driver. Throughout the world, countless numbers of children are brought from their homes to school and safely returned by millions of drivers. The bus ride can be a wonderful way to begin each day when the driver greets the children warmly, keeps the activity in the bus positive, and safely drives to school. At the end of school, the bus driver returns the children, setting the tone for the rest of the day. The driver can make the beginning and end of the day something life enhancing. When done with love and respect, driving a school bus makes a profoundly positive impact on millions of children every day.

If the bus driver does not have compassion for his or her riders, the impact is also profound. The beginning and ending of each school day become times of punishment. Rules are not enforced, leading to some children teasing others. Bullying can occur, making the bus a place of torment for an unpopular child. The noise level can go beyond reason, adding more chaos to a bad situation. It may be that no talking is allowed, robbing the children of the opportunity to deepen friendships. Children learn from their driver that their very presence is inconvenient, that they are nuisances that must be endured rather than gifts to be treasured. Because the driver governs one of the earliest places that children go without their parents, his or her actions can teach them something profound about the world beyond their homes: that the world holds great love and promise or that the world is dangerous and belittling. Such is the power of the bus driver's work.

When given some thought, the same implications arise from many occupations rarely thought of as important. While the worth of physicians, social workers, ministers, lawyers, and judges is obvious to most people, the worth of others is not. The working life of a partner or spouse is an opportunity to have a ministry that has profound implications for the world. Recognition for a job well done, for a unique contribution to the life of the world, for a ministry, is vital. Who knows the full implications of anyone's work? Only God. Still, the spouse or partner can trust that when a baptismal call is answered through work, the value is beyond calculation.

The career of a spouse or partner may also provide a way for answering a profound question: Who am I called to be? What a partner does for work should have a deep connection to who he or she is. What a spouse spends time doing should lead to a greater sense of self as a person of faith. While work does not reveal the fullness of anyone, it can deepen or deaden the spiritual life. God calls all people to become holy in a larger sense. The working out of a career can deepen the spiritual life of a spouse. When a partner's work is done as a baptismal ministry, the spirit of the partner becomes ever more truly reflective of God's love for the world while also becoming uniquely himself or herself.

There is no single way to live a life of faith, and there is more than one way for a person to grow in faith. For one partner, an occupation becomes a place to deepen self-understanding; for another, it may be merely a means to an end. For a particular person, careers may change throughout life. In some locations or for some span of time, an occupation may enrich the faith life and identity of a partner. In other places and times, it may drain a spouse of emotional, physical, and spiritual energy. The question of self-identity, the "who am I" that all people must ask, is related to the work of our hands, for better and for worse.

It is obvious, in his or her work, that a spouse or partner is an individual, not an appendage of the ordained other half. For many partners and spouses, work is the environment that expects and affirms an identity separate from the ordained ministry. The partner is not just the shadow of the minister; the spouse is not a detached third arm without hopes, dreams, gifts, and needs. When a spouse or partner feels unseen and unappreciated because of the ordained ministry of a covenant partner, work may be the only place that affirms a separate (though not unrelated) identity. Through relocation, loss of community, and life changes, the work of a spouse or partner may provide a constant in the midst of change. It is valuable and valued.

With these thoughts it mind, a question arises: what about the time factor? As noted earlier, the clergy wives in the Morris and Blanton study found that time was a critical factor in their parental satisfaction and in their overall life satisfaction.[11] When work responsibilities, family demands, and church duties became a burden, satisfaction with life ebbed. It is possible that even a positive work experience can lead to higher levels of stress because of the time it requires. Resentment toward church obligations and family duties left unmet tinge time at work with a darker element. The wife may resent the time spent away from family and faith community. This can be true if the wife is in the husband's community, another church, or in another faith tradition entirely. Always being short on time means always trying to catch up. There is no end to the race, and no reward at the end of the workday or workweek. It is an exhausting existence with no end in sight. If this is reality for a clergy wife, it is critical that she seek help. The clergy husband must review his own work expectations in light of his wife's life pace. If the expectations of a church community can only be met through a spouse's soul-sucking schedule, those expectations need to be confronted and changed. Courage is needed for clergy couples to admit to the time squeeze, and bravery for them to set a good example for others by refusing to answer the siren call of workaholism.

What about the male partners and spouses of clergy marriages? Do they feel the same time constraints as their female counterparts? When a female pastor leads a congregation, is her husband expected to participate in the leadership of the church? These are vital questions that have not been addressed yet. There is precious little research on clergy marriages and unions of any sort, and even less on husbands and male partners of ministers. While the study cited noted that the ordained husbands found intrusiveness the critical factor in their overall life satisfaction, time was not as critical. Would this be true of men who are partners or spouses, or would time become a critical indicator of overall life satisfaction? As the number of female clergy increases, serious research on this issue is needed. At present, a few things for consideration will have to suffice.

GENDER DIFFERENCES AND EXPECTATIONS

It may be that women feel more pressured by lack of time because they are responsible for the many demands of child care, housework, and keeping the family schedule. Feelings of guilt and inadequacy may arise for women because they do more work within the family than their male partners. If the traditional way of raising children and maintaining a household are followed in a clergy marriage or union, the male spouse or partner may not experience the time crunch to the same extent because the ordained woman is still responsible for the running of house and family.[12] This still leaves the intrusiveness factor, which affects both men and women in their overall life satisfaction.

In reference to the three areas of work—family, church, personal career—are the male spouses and partners expected to fulfill the roles that clergy wives do? Many congregations who hire female clergy are in new territory, so the entrenched expectations for the spouse or partner may be questioned. Community members may assume that the male partner will have his own career to tend, and that he will not be available to be an unpaid assistant. The relationship between the congregation and the spouse may be something that can be developed over time; it may be something entirely new for the congregation, and this newness may allow the male partner to set parameters for involvement that help to reduce the intrusive nature of the ministry.

Does this mean that the female partners of ordained ministers have fewer choices while also having more defined expectations from the community? Perhaps. Male and female spouses and partners have choices, but the female spouse may find that making those choices requires more effort than it does for a male spouse. This is unfair, but true for many spouses. In most churches that have married clergy, there have been female spouses from the beginning. The male spouse is something new to most denominations, entering into faith communities without established expectations. The female minister is the one challenging the historic picture of ministry, and she will bear the greatest burden in challenging entrenched expectations. This may leave her partner free to set new parameters for his relationship with the faith community. This is exciting, but comes with the added responsibility of knowing that future spouses and partners will be affected by the parameters set.[13]

Whatever work a spouse or partner chooses to do, it should be valued. If it is the working out of a baptismal ministry, if it is a means to financial solvency, or if it is both, the "second" career is a vital element in the lives of spouses and their clergy halves. Making sure that both in the covenant relationship honor that work and respect its integrity is a way to honor the value of a spouse. God created partners, both male and female, and their work can be something good for their union, their faith journeys, and for the world at large. There is nothing "second" about that.

EXERCISES FOR WORK DISCERNMENT

What work is meaningful to me? For the spouse or partner, this question is not necessarily integral to the working life. He or she may be working in a particular field because it is meaningful. On the other hand, a particular job or profession may have been chosen for convenience and financial benefit only. Adapting a secular career around the needs of ordination often begins with a geographical relocation for seminary studies. The partner takes a job that is available and able to provide sufficient money and benefits to support the family. The spouse may give up not only a particular position to support his or her clergy half, but may give up a whole line of work. If the preferred line of work cannot be found where the other half is studying, positions in other fields may be the only way to pay the bills. This loss may be temporary, if the spouse can find work in a chosen career during the seminary study years or soon afterward. The loss may be permanent if the partner cannot find a position in a particular field in a new location. It takes three years to earn a Master's of Divinity, the degree required for ordination in most denominations.

In the United Church of Christ, the typical four-year bachelor's degree and three-year MDiv degree before ordination is not the only model available. Depending upon the individual situation, a person can be licensed to serve as a minister before completing his or her years of education. A person may be commissioned for ministry that does not require ordination but involves an active ministry in congregational, educational, or denominational settings. Whether these alternatives to the traditional pathway to ordained ministry bring the same issues depends upon the specific circumstances involved.[14]

After graduation, the newly ordained half may be limited in where a call to a church may be taken. The partner may end up tailoring his or her work life around these geographical restrictions. Does the search for meaningful work end because of these restrictions? How can a partner go about seeking meaning in the working life?

It begins by asking questions. While the process of ordination encourages, even requires, asking and answering such questions, a spouse may not know where or how to begin asking the questions.[15] The first question, the most difficult, will be asked throughout a lifetime: what work is meaningful to me? Answering this question will require time and attention. Prayer and meditation can provide a wider context for pondering the meaning of daily work. A journal to track thoughts, questions, observances, and answers can provide a tangible basis for this quest. Creating collages, listening to music, working with words can help a spouse or partner focus on what is most meaningful about work. To answer this question, other questions may arise. Some of these are obvious, some not. These questions can help a partner articulate the meaningful nature of work, or may lead a spouse to seek work that is meaningful. The following two exercises can help.

Exercise One: Is My Work Intrinsically Meaningful?

Write this question at the top of a blank piece of paper. Write a short answer to this question as a starting place. Continue to think about the meaning of work by adding details to these statements:

- I am doing something that has personal meaning for me and gives something to the world.[16]
- I foster the lives of others by doing my work well.
- I take pride in my work.
- I can see my gifts grow through work.[17]

For many people, there are few opportunities to reflect on how work fosters personal growth for an individual and also how it benefits the larger community. For a spouse, placing his or her work into this larger context can be the beginning of a new way to understand and appreciate daily toil. There are direct benefits that come from the labor of most people, to the worker and to those who live in the community. When a partner spends time and energy reflecting on the implications of work, it can lead to a greater appreciation for that work. It may also lead to greater satisfaction at work. This exercise cannot be done properly in a few minutes. Returning to these statements over a span of weeks, perhaps setting aside an hour every week for this exercise, will lead to a deeper understanding of how work affects a partner's individual life, the life of the family, and the life of the world.

The second part of this exercise is for the clergy half of the marriage or union. He or she may not spend a lot of time thinking about the spouse's work. To develop a greater appreciation for the labor of the nonordained partner, the clergy half should answer the first question and elaborate on the three statements, changing the "I" to "my partner." This can keep both informed about the other's work and foster a greater appreciation for the labor of both. There is more to work than a paycheck, and more to the working life of covenant partners than the hours spent on it.

This exercise can be helpful for those spouses and partners who do not work for a paycheck. If the covenant couple configures life around one career rather than two, the work done within the home, in ministry, and in volunteer tasks can be reviewed. The unpaid work done by a spouse may involve a lot of time and many skills that make a quality life possible for a covenant couple. It is worth the time to find out just how valuable the work of a "nonworking" spouse is. This can be done by listing the tasks involved and estimating their cost if provided by an outside agency. For example, parents who stay home and do not use full time daycare or nursery care facilities save a lot of money. The same can be calculated for cooking, cleaning, and other household tasks. For volunteer work, assigning a value based upon a comparable career can help estimate the economic gain for the community. The idea is not to calculate the exact value, but to look at the unpaid work as something vital to the life of the couple, family, and larger community. This exercise can help covenant partners gain a new appreciation for the work of both.[18]

Exercise Two: How Does My Work Add to the Quality of My Life and the Lives of Those around Me?

The work of a spouse or partner has its intrinsic value, as explored in the first exercise. It also has an indirect value because it generates income (or lowers expenses if it is unpaid). Write a short answer to this question, and elaborate on the following statements:

- My work contributes to the well-being of my life and my family's life.[19]
- I set a good example of financial responsibility.
- I bring a larger perspective into my marriage or union because of my work.
- My work supports my partner's ministry.
- My partner supports me in my work and in my ministry.

As with the first exercise, this exercise is designed to bring a larger perspective and a deeper appreciation for the partner's work. It is a wonderful exercise for both within the union to do, for their own work and that of their spouse. Taking the time to write on these statements and questions, and taking the time to reflect on the answers as individuals and as a couple, can make the interplay between both careers more visible. With a greater understanding of how the working lives of both partners interact, new possibilities arise.

The clarity that comes from these exercises may prompt one or both partners to reconsider their work lives. If the spouse or partner comes to the conclusion that a change needs to be made, these exercises can help set the stage for that change. If the ordained spouse sees his or her ministry in the context of the partner's work, an openness and flexibility in how the call to ministry is answered may result. For both, a greater appreciation for their own labor and the work of their partner may arise. This is one way for each to see the other as an equal, giving both a fresh appreciation for how their working lives are lived out within their relationship.

Taking a long look at how the baptismal ministries of both partners are being lived out through work is not easy. It requires effort and intent, and neither can claim ignorance of the other's situation as an excuse to avoid change. Feelings of resentment may surface along with a greater understanding of and appreciation for work. If these exercises end in profound conflict, it may be necessary to seek a therapist, career counselor, or pastoral counselor. Clarity can open up new possibilities for both, but it also shines a light on entrenched practices and assumptions that uphold the value of one partner's work at the expense of the other. With patience, humor, and guidance when necessary, both will have the opportunity to live lives of greater depth. Whether the deepening arises from the appreciation for the present way of working, or if it comes from making some changes, it is well worth the effort involved.

WHOSE TURN IS IT?

Relocation is not an annual event, but it is usually part of a minister's career.[20] A pastor may move from a small church to a larger one, or from an assistant position in one church to a solo pastorate in another. These changes are not promotions in the sense that one ministry is more vital than another, but may be the way to earn more money and gain greater prestige among colleagues. In some denominations, a minister is moved from church to church with very little say in the timing or location. Sometimes these moves are local, keeping the family within a specific state or geographic area. In other denominations, the moves may not be required, but may involve moving into different regions of the country, or to other countries. In previous pages, the stress that is caused by relocation has been reviewed. Now the focus is on how relocation affects the working life of a spouse or partner. If the couple decides to move to a new place, how is this decision made? Whose job takes priority, and how is that decision made? Do the covenant partners maintain a sense of fairness in their career decisions, giving the other's career equal consideration? If both are committed to their work, whose career governs the moves, and whose career must accommodate? Do both partners get a turn?

Moving for Ministry

When a minister changes his or her job, there is almost always relocation involved. For many reasons, ministers are not encouraged or not allowed to move from an assistant's position in a particular church to the head of staff position. Ministers seeking another church to serve are not encouraged and sometimes not allowed to remain in the same town.[21] While many do remain in the same geographical area, others take positions far away from their previous church locations. This continues the pattern of relocation that began with seminary studies and the first ordained ministry.

In the Morris and Blanton study, the participating couples had relocated three or four times over a seventeen-year period, making a move every five to seven years.[22] Because this survey focused on the ordained ministry, there is no data on the number of positions that the spouses left. There is no information on how many left one line of work for another because of the relocations for ministry. What is clear is that a spouse or partner will have to change his or her working location if the couple moves from one area to another. If a partner continually changes from one profession to another, or moves from one company to another within the same field, his or her financial future is affected. Benefits and retirement funds may not be transferred from one place to another. Constant relocation affects promotions and salaries that are based upon seniority and a proven record of competency. When a career of a spouse or partner is consistently modified to adapt to the itinerant nature of ordained ministry, it suffers.[23] Moving may be something that a spouse or partner accepts with little difficulty, or it may be a source of constant resentment. In either case, it has a profound effect on the partner's working life.

When a minister's call to a new position governs a relocation, there are always implications for the partner's work. For a spouse who understands his or her work as secondary to other aspects of life, the implications may be inconvenient but not deeply troubling. The partner may work in a career that allows great mobility, such as teaching in public school or nursing. Rather than depend upon a company retirement plan, a spouse can establish personal retirement funds. This takes intentional effort, but it is possible. The partner is then the one with the "second career," following whatever path the ordained ministry career sets.

For a partner whose career is of primary importance, either because it is a way to live out a baptismal calling or because it is central to his or her identity, moving to accommodate ordained ministry has some grave implications. For careers that are specific to certain locations, a move may mean that there are no opportunities to work. For a corporate career, relocation may mean leaving one company and starting again at another. The spouse may earn a decent salary because of past experience, but will lose tenure and career stability. It takes time to earn promotions, to move from being the newcomer to a trusted member of an established team.

With every new relocation, the spouse may become less appealing to employers. If it is clear that he or she will not remain in the area for more than a few years, an employer may not give a spouse a chance. When the length of time at a certain position is set by another's career, an employer may question the value of the partner's work. These are not judgments made because of a lack of ability, but due to parameters that are outside the working relationship for the spouse and the employer. The partner may be hired for positions that do not reflect his or her abilities within a field. Tenure becomes tenuous. The spouse may be serious about a career, but still end up sacrificing seniority and interesting work because of the reality of the ordained ministry. It is difficult to be a serious career person and be a committed covenant partner with someone whose call to ministry involves regular relocation.

Moving for the Partner's Career

While the Morris and Blanton study did not address the issue of clergy couples who relocate for the nonordained partner's career, this is an option. Some ordained ministers tailor their careers around their spouse's work, finding a ministry within the geographic parameters set by a nonordained position. For those partners pursuing a career in which promotion is tied to relocation, a move may be necessary to move up. The spouse's employment may be more flexible when it comes to moving because it may be possible to commute from some distance away rather than live in the same town as the workplace. This means that the ordained partner may have a wider radius of opportunity in which to seek a position. The covenant couple can set specific parameters for commuting that address the work needs of both.

When the nonordained career prompts a move, there are several factors that must be considered. If no ordained ministry is immediately found, can the couple live on one salary? If not, is the minister willing to work outside full-time ministry temporarily?[24] Does the spouse's career have a stable retirement and benefits package, providing not only a current salary but future financial security? Is this relocation for a short period of time, or a permanent move? Are there opportunities for an ordained ministry at the location, if not immediately then in the future? Is the job satisfaction that comes from the relocation worth it for all involved?

Taking Turns

If the demands of two careers conflict, is it possible to take turns, allowing one partner's career to dictate some moves and not others? This can be a way of honoring both the lay and ordained work of both, but it has its complications. On the positive side, it allows both partners to seek meaningful work, and shows that both take the work of the other seriously. When the ordained ministry dictates a move, the spouse supports it by relocating. When the partner's nonordained work requires relocation, the minister seeks work within the field at a new location. The willingness of both to sacrifice for the other shows that there is a sense of equality in the relationship, and that one does not consider the other an extension of his or her work. Both have their individual work affirmed in tangible ways, and both bear the costs of accommodating a career to the other's work. The careers of both are modified in light of the other and in light of the needs of the family. If both are people of faith, then the work of both becomes a way to live out two baptismal ministries. Lay work that comes out of the baptismal gifts of the nonordained partner is seen as a profoundly faithful way of life, and so is the ordained ministry. The careers of both are placed in a larger context, one that considers the importance of each and how both affect the faith lives of all involved.

There are some concerns in switching the priority from one career to the other. The most obvious is the issue of building up a solid financial base. Retirement benefits require steady work over a span of years. If a career stops and starts, then less is invested in the retirement plans provided by either career.[25] This is true of Social Security benefits, too, which are based upon the cumulative work done by an individual. One partner's position may provide health benefits while the other's does not. If one partner's retirement benefits end when he or she dies, then the surviving partner may need a separate and adequate income beyond what Social Security provides. Unless the covenant couple can save for their future financial needs in ways not connected to their professions, taking turns by alternating whose career takes priority may be unrealistic.

In addition to the financial difficulties involved, there are issues of timing. There must be positions available for one or both of the people involved, and those positions have to be reliable. The job market has to be favorable to the partner whose career is taking priority. If there are opportunities for one spouse and not the other, then there may be times when taking turns isn't a matter of switching career priorities every other move. The lives of all involved must be considered, and career opportunities for both must be available for this "every other time" alternating pattern. In a perfect world, career opportunities come along at the right time and in the right place. In reality, things may not be so neat. Compromises must be made and equality maintained not in a regimented fashion, but in an overall sense.

Whose Career Accommodates?

If taking turns is not a possibility, then one career must be adapted to the other. This does not mean that only one career is important, but that the covenant couple realizes that financial reality and available opportunities will modify their work plans. If both are committed to each other, then both must work together to resolve the inevitable conflicts that two careers generate in a relationship. Both partners must be flexible, immediate and long-term financial issues considered, the value of relocation questioned, and the larger context in which both pursue their careers acknowledged. Both the minister and the nonordained partner must decide which factors are important when one career is pursued at the expense of another. Should the profession that brings the greatest financial reward take priority? If one partner's work has a critical significance for a particular time and place, is it more important? Each couple must agree upon the factors that affect which career takes top billing at any one point in time. If one career takes priority over the other as a general rule, then both should agree that it is for the benefit of all involved. The following points and questions can initiate a conversation about career issues and bring clarity into the ongoing relationship between the working lives of the two in covenant relationship.

Both Partners Must Be Flexible

The careers of both have value, but neither partner is defined solely in terms of his or her career. The working lives of both must be put into the larger context of their lives, for they are vital elements but should not be definitive. Both must be willing to give priority to the other's career. The following questions should be considered by both when career opportunities arise: Am I willing to give up sole focus on my career so that my spouse can find meaningful work? Is my partner willing to put my career needs first? Can one or both careers be reenvisioned to allow both to flourish in different circumstances? Is there more than one way for me to serve God and the world through work, lay or ordained?

FINANCIAL REALITY: PROVIDING FOR CURRENT AND FUTURE NEEDS

Is it necessary for both partners to work, regardless of whose career takes priority? Is one salary more important than the other, providing benefits and a sustainable life that the other cannot? If one salary is significantly larger than the other, does it always take priority? If it does, should it? Is it possible to live on one salary if both find that appealing? If one partner dies, what are the financial ramifications? It is not possible to anticipate all future financial needs, nor is it possible to insure that present needs will not change in unexpected ways. These questions must be revisited and the work situation occasionally reevaluated to make sure that both partners are satisfied with the financial decisions being made.

THE VALUE OF RELOCATION

The professional, full-time ordained ministry usually requires moving from one situation to another. Most move every few years, and clergy families should consider the impact relocation has upon everyone involved before packing the boxes. Certain secular professions also require relocation, creating the same situation. Some questions about a new location center upon financial realities. Couples must ask themselves these questions while considering a particular move: Can we live in this location, or is it too costly? Are both of us required to work full-time in order to survive in a particular location? If so, is this desirable? Are there other options available? Are there work opportunities for both of us in this place? Do we know how a move will affect our standard of living?

When considering a move, whether for the ordained career or the partner's career, there are factors beyond finance that must be considered. Both partners should ask themselves these questions, and both should take seriously the hopes and reservations of the other *before* any move is made. These are critical questions: Is this move necessary? Why or why not? Is this specific move desirable? How will this relocation help us as we live in covenant relationship? How will it help us live out our baptismal ministries? What happens if we stay where we are? If there are children in the family, additional questions arise: Will this move be good for everyone in the long run? Is this a difficult time to move for some members of the family?[26] If this is a relocation for financial gain only, is it worth the cost to the overall quality of life?

CONSIDERING THE LARGER CONTEXT

Relocating for career advancement is not an automatic step, because a career does not govern all aspects of life. No one should reduce life to work, no matter how important it might be to the individual or the larger world. Before a couple decides to relocate for career reasons, the larger life context must be considered. If both place their work in the context of their religious beliefs, then each move must be evaluated on its merits as a ministry. Do both partners feel that God is best served by a move? Is this move a way for the faith lives of all involved to flourish? Is it the only option, the best option, or the most faithful response to Christ's call to serve the world? Will a particular move at a particular time be damaging to one or more members of the family?

When a couple moves for career reasons, even with careful thought and planning, the situation can be something quite different from what was expected. If one partner finds that the situation is unacceptable, the other must take it seriously. Before a move is made, the couple should consider this possibility. If a situation becomes untenable for one or both, what is the next step? Can a limited amount of time be spent in a location that does not bring positive experiences for all involved? Is there an escape clause in effect, allowing one or both partners to create a back-up plan? No one moves to a location with the expectation that things will turn out badly, but there should be an agreement between the partners that either can initiate a departure plan if a situation becomes unacceptable. This is not a simple process, nor is it something that can be done in a few weeks or even months. It takes time to adjust to a new situation, and time to justify a negative opinion about that situation. It will take time to leave a position and a community. Keeping both careers in the larger context of their lives as individuals, as a covenant couple, and as part of a larger family and community allows the spouses to recognize a bad situation and prompts both to change that situation as quickly and responsibly as possible.

Keeping an eye on the larger context is a matter of discussion and cooperation; it is also a matter of discernment. Prayerful discussion and continuous prayer help both the ordained minister and the lay partner ask for guidance and make decisions based upon more than a salary and job satisfaction. Life is so much richer than a work experience, and a work experience can enrich life. Holding both these truths together, and holding them together for both partners, is critical to living in a covenant relationship and honoring the working lives of both.

REENVISIONING THE LOCATION OF MINISTRY AND SECULAR WORK

Future work is not chiseled in stone, but written in the heart. When relocation demands the sacrifice of one workplace, even of a career, it may lead to significant work as yet unknown. If the decision to move has been made by both covenant partners, why not use the opportunity to rethink a working life? It may lead to new appreciation of a current career; it may lead to something entirely new. It is a sacrifice to give up meaningful work, but it is also an opportunity to dream new career dreams.

When two careers must be coordinated, both partners must be flexible. Both must affirm the importance of the other's work, and both must be willing to reconsider assumptions about what a career should look like. This is as true of an ordained ministry as it is of secular work. There are many ways to live out a baptismal calling, either through a career or through meaningful work outside of a career. There are also many ways to live out a call to ordination when that call is understood as a particular way to live out Christ's call to follow. When considering a career move that entails a geographical move, both partners should question the assumptions that they have about their working lives. What are the key elements of each partner's work that make it a gift to God and the world? Are there other careers or other ministries that also have these key elements? Do both partners wish to continue working the amount they currently work, or is a new configuration of working life a goal?[27] Asking these questions and taking the time to answer them may break open the expectations that both have for their work lives. New ideas and new opportunities may be considered, and a wider vision of how their careers are lived out may result.

When an ordained minister thinks about ministry, it is often in a congregational setting. Serving a church as the solo pastor or as part of a larger staff is the most common ordained ministry. It is not the only way. In addition to congregational or parish settings, ordained ministers serve as hospital chaplains, prison chaplains, and campus chaplains for university and private schools. Ordained ministers also work for denominational offices, nonprofit organizations, as teachers in seminaries and other locations, as camp directors, as pastoral counselors, and as spiritual directors. There are many ways to live out a call to ordained ministry, and each is a way to serve Christ and the world. The contours of the working life will change from one setting to another, offering more than one option to clergy and their spouses. The schedules and the number of hours required vary from location to location and from ministry to ministry. For example, a hospital chaplain may work a nine-to-five workweek with regularly scheduled overnight "on-call" weekends. A prison chaplain may lead services on weekends but work very few nights. Campus chaplaincies may require living on campus, teaching religious studies classes, and spending time with students in the evenings. If a minister can serve Christ in meaningful ways in multiple settings, it allows for greater flexibility for his or her partner and the "second career." Recognizing and being open to more than one kind of ordained ministry can allow a minister to live more fully into covenant relationship because the needs of the spouse or partner can be considered and met.

When a couple changes location for a new ordained ministry, whether this is the permanent pattern in the relationship, an every-other-move occurrence, or a once in a lifetime event, the career of the spouse or partner will be affected. In the best of circumstances, a partner finds work in his or her field in the new location, experiencing very little career upheaval. At times, a spouse may lose seniority at a particular company, but is able to find work in the same field; adjustments are made, but a positive work experience results. Sometimes, no options exist in the partner's chosen field of work. If the partner feels called to this secular work, either as a ministry or as a way to give back something to the world that has nothing to do with religious faith, this can be heartbreaking. If both within the covenant feel that the move is the right step, then the spouse must reenvision the working life to adapt to the new situation. But how is this done?

As a first step, the partner and the ordained half should recognize the sacrifice that is involved: a spouse is giving up a work life so that a ministry can be pursued. That cost needs to be acknowledged and appreciated by both because one is bearing the burden of lost career opportunities. The ordained half may shoulder greater financial responsibility with the move, but his or her professional life is the primary focus. This sets the context for their lives together for years to come. The decision to move should not be made lightly, nor should it be made against the express wishes of a partner or spouse. Both must make the decision, not just one. Both partners should drive into the new location without harboring deep resentment, and with hope that the needs of both will be met.

If there is no chance of working in his or her chosen field, the partner must reenvision the working life. To do this, questions should be asked: what matters to me most in my work life? What are the elements of my career that appeal to me? Can those be found in other work situations? Is this move an opportunity to try something new? Is pursuing additional education appealing and possible? What dreams are made possible by this new situation? What brings me the greatest joy and satisfaction in my work? How do I see myself serving God and the world from this particular location in this time of my life? The answers to these questions may lead to unexpected opportunities and new career goals. They may lead a spouse back to his or her former career. In either case, a new adventure begins.

WHEN A COUPLE HITS AN IMPASSE

What happens when one of the covenant partners wants to pursue a career opportunity that the other is against? What is the next step when one is unwilling to accommodate the career needs and aspirations of the other? How can the couple continue to have fruitful conversation about their work lives?

One reason why couples hit a roadblock is that the two hold different values when it comes to work. Does the larger salary control the location of work? Does the fact that ordination is a "call" from God make it the most important career, regardless of financial gain? Is it assumed that the man's career takes priority over the woman's, regardless of other factors? Are there outside issues affecting the choice of career location?[28] Is it important for one of the partners to be free from full-time work responsibilities in order to focus on family life or other meaningful, unpaid work?[29] Is a particular work situation appealing because it offers the opportunity for personal growth and financial gain? Whose work life bears the biggest cost of a move? Whose career benefits from the move? All of these questions should be answered by both partners so that both can understand why they are at an impasse.

What comes out of a deep and honest conversation is a sense of each other's perspective. What values are serving as the basis for career decisions? In a clash of values and priorities, hard decisions must be made. Each must be willing to sacrifice something for the other because that keeps a sense of equality and fairness in the conversation and in the relationship. Without mutual respect and a willingness to sacrifice for the other, the impasse ends in one partner winning and the other losing. Sacrifice for one another is not a matter of winning or losing, but of mutual respect and accommodation. There is a cost but the fundamental equality of both remains, along with respect and affection. In contrast, there is no fundamental equality when one partner's win forces the other partner's loss. The sacrifice of one partner's career for the other, in a short-term situation or over a longer period of time, is something willingly undertaken. When it is forced, it is not sacrifice but oppression. This ends in bitterness within the union and may well kill the union. The couple may continue to live together but will not be living in covenant.

Each covenant marriage or union is unique, with its own context and equilibrium. Each is lived in relationship to God and the larger world. Each covenant holds both partners together, calling them to mutual care and respect. When the two involved hit a career impasse, both must ask themselves these questions: Is my job my identity? Do I value my partner's work as equal to mine? Can I compromise without bitterness?

Whenever two people enter into a union or marriage, profound differences of opinion arise, unexpected needs and assumptions appear, and the future holds possibilities and challenges not yet thought of. Without a sense of equality, without a larger context for the work of both, and without a willingness to sacrifice for the other, the impasse will move from a career issue to a profoundly personal one. Winning the career game is not the goal for either because someone must lose. Meaningful work, whether it is secular or baptismal or ordained, cannot bring good things into a covenant relationship unless it is done with the willing sacrifice of both partners.

The career aspirations of a spouse or partner are not to be taken lightly, nor are they to be considered less important than the ministry aspirations of the ordained partner. While the couple may agree that the nonordained career is the "second" career for a multitude of reasons, it is not second in the sense that it is less important. How the working life of a partner is perceived by both within the relationship can be a gauge for their marriage covenant. If there is a shared sense of equality, then the work lives of both inform and deepen their common life. If the work of one is deemed of more value than the other, it may indicate that one partner is valued over the other. However the work lives of the couple are configured, it is vital that each appreciate his or her own work and that of the partner. What value is given to the spouse's secular work cannot damage a union when a fundamental equality exists. Both will sacrifice, both will support, and both may find the work of their hands a holy undertaking.

No matter how much we value our work, we remain more than our working selves. Who we are is valued by God and should be valued by a partner more than any career—lay or ordained. When the demands of two careers are in conflict, this central truth can help a couple find the blessing in the struggle.

Four

House and Home

Our first church provided a home. It was attached to the church building and had a door that led from the church hall to our kitchen. I remember being awakened early one morning to strange sounds coming from our kitchen. When I went downstairs, a church member was going through my cupboards. She said, "You don't mind me borrowing an extra pot, do you?" She had used the sexton's key to unlock the connecting door.

The parsonage was always a mess. When the pastor and family left, it took days to clean out the house. The damage done to the walls, ceilings, and porch was way beyond normal wear. It cost thousands of dollars to get the house back in decent shape!

People from the church would drop by the house at all hours, without calling first. It didn't matter if it was my wife's day off, they had no respect for our privacy.

None of us ever saw the inside of the minister's house. He expected us to invite him and his family into our homes, but he never invited anyone into his.[1]

When a minister takes a call to serve a church, a move to a new house is usually involved. Most churches expect their pastor to live near the church, sharing in the life of the wider community as well as the life of their congregation. Some churches provide a house as part of the minister's compensation package. Other congregations offer a *housing allowance,* a specific amount of money designated for the cost of housing. In other places, churches may make special housing arrangements for the clergy and their partners. There are advantages and disadvantages to each of these housing options, and they affect the lives of all involved. How do the various housing arrangements help in creating a welcoming home for ministers, spouses and partners, and children? What are the implications of church-owned housing rather than buying a home? These questions, and how the answers affect the family, are the focus of this chapter. There are examples of how spouses and partners have created a home for themselves and their mates throughout this chapter. May these provide inspiration for creating nurturing homes in many different housing situations!

PROVIDED HOUSING: MANSE, PARSONAGE, RECTORY

Some churches provide their ministers with housing. Depending upon the denomination and geographical location, these houses can be called *manses, parsonages,* or *rectories.* They come in all shapes, sizes, and conditions. Some are literally attached to the church. Others are located on the same site. Some are close to the church, but not on the same street. Houses can be located within a few hundred yards of the church or may be found anywhere within the community the church serves. In churches with large grounds and multiple staff members, there may be several houses or apartments that serve to house clergy.

When a church sends information about the community and the terms of financial compensation to a prospective minister, usually there is a space somewhere in the paperwork labeled "housing"; a term such as "provided," or one of the terms listed above, will be in the "housing" space.[2] The church information form might also list the value of the provided housing. For example, if a church in Boston provides a three-bedroom apartment for their minister, the market value could be listed as $3,000 dollars a month or more. This would be the cost of renting it if it were not provided. In this case, the housing value would be $36,000 per year, not including utilities. This figure would be included in the total amount of financial compensation offered to the minister.

There are many benefits to church-provided housing. One of the most obvious is that there is no house hunting involved. If the couple is not familiar with the area, this takes away the burden of finding a house. The couple has information about the size of the house, the number of rooms it has, whether it is partially furnished, and the window dimensions for ordering or making curtains. The size of the yard is also known, making it easier to decide what to bring to the new house, what to leave behind, and what might be necessary to purchase for upkeep.

A second advantage to this housing arrangement is that it is similar to renting a home. Major repairs to the house and property, assuming that the minister and family did not do unreasonable damage, are the responsibility of the church. If the house is located on church grounds, yard maintenance may also be provided. If the minister's denomination requires frequent relocations, the minister and partner do not have to worry about selling a house. Whatever the condition of the real estate market, neither the church nor the couple need worry about buying or selling a house.

Parsonages, rectories, and manses are almost always located near the church, making for a quick commute. If the house or apartment is not located on the church grounds, it is often within walking distance, or at most a few miles away. The advantage to this is in time and money saved. Working as a minister demands a great deal of time and energy, making a short commute a great advantage. Having a house close to work means that less money will be spent on fuel and other travel costs.

Another advantage to housing provided by the church is its affordability. Because housing expense is a large portion of the overall cost of living, a provided house or apartment makes it financially possible for ministers to live in the communities they serve without needing to purchase or rent housing beyond their means. This is also an advantage to the church community; the cost of providing a house may be much less expensive than providing an adequate cash allowance for housing a minister. If a particular minister chooses to purchase a home rather than live in the parsonage, the church can rent the property to offset the cost of providing a monetary housing allowance.

Having a house provided by a church may not be as vital if the salary and housing allowance for the minister is in the median range of the income for residents in that area. For example, if the median income of residents in a particular town is $56,000 per year, a minister and spouse earning $65,000 per year may be able to buy a house without incurring unreasonable debt.

But if the median income of residents in a particular town is $250,000 per year and a minister and partner earn $65,000, buying a house in the community may be impossible. When a house is provided, it becomes possible for the couple to live in a community whose residents earn more than they do.[3]

For the partner and his or her clergy half, there are some disadvantages to church-provided housing. The first is that there is no choice in the type of house or its grounds. The house or apartment is a specific size and style, regardless of the tastes of the spouse and minister. It may be too big for the needs of the couple, or too small for a large family. The grounds may require too much maintenance or be inappropriate for children. Changes may be made to the house, but those changes are not the sole decision of the couple. As with renting a house, there are parameters for change that limit what can and cannot be done to the house and property.

A second possible disadvantage is the location of the housing. The couple has no choice in this matter, whether it is on the church grounds or not. One couple may like living next to the church while others want some distance from the church buildings. Unless the church has more than one option for housing, the couple must accept the location of the housing as part of the reality of serving the church. This will affect the spouse or partner's commute, should he or she work. If there are children, it means attending whatever public school serves the town.[4]

When a couple lives in provided housing rather than buying a house, there is a financial cost. As with renting, provided housing does not give the couple the opportunity to build up equity in a house. This is not a short-term disadvantage because it does not affect the daily finances of the couple. However, it is a serious disadvantage for their financial future. Owning a home provides long-term financial security as an eventually rent free home or as a substantial amount of money from its sale. The equity in a home can also be used to secure college or business loans, should they be needed. The money spent on mortgage payments provides the couple with financial security rather than just a place to live.

Some churches may offset this disadvantage for the couple by providing an *equity allowance*. A specific sum of money is provided for the couple in place of the equity that they would build if they owned a home. The couple can invest this money for later use, or can use it to purchase another property. This makes up for the financial disadvantage of living in provided housing. It requires careful planning by the couple and a church with the ability to offer the equity allowance.

The fourth concern centers on making changes to the housing provided. Because the couple does not own the house or apartment, there may be constraints on any changes made to its appearance, both inside and outside. The community members responsible for the house's upkeep may object to painting the rooms of the house in anything other than white or other neutral shades. Stenciling or painting murals may be a passion for the family, but a headache for the church. Can the kitchen be painted and papered in an apple theme? Is a vegetable garden allowed if the house is located in the church's backyard? Is it acceptable to work on old cars in the driveway? If the couple has a dog, can an area of the yard be fenced in? Can a hammock be put up between the trees off the back of the house? What about the neon green and yellow wading pool? These questions, both serious and silly, can damage the relationship between the church community and the couple if they are not addressed to the satisfaction of everyone.

The church community may also experience some disadvantages of providing housing for their ministers. The upkeep of a house requires an ongoing investment of time and money. If the house is old, repairing the leaking roof and replacing draughty windows are costly. If lead paint or asbestos were used in the house, removal is the responsibility of the church community. Heating systems and wiring must be kept up to date, and carpets replaced every so many years. When a minister is not living in the house, the church is still responsible for it. Someone must attend to renting the property if it is financially necessary. The church becomes the landlord for anyone who lives in the house—minister and family, or occasional renter.

When it comes to housing, each church community must decide what is best for the community and for the ministers who will serve it. The situation changes with each new minister because the community changes over time, the real estate values of the larger community change, the financial situation of the church changes, and the housing needs change. Offering a housing allowance may have been impossible in past years, but advantageous to all involved at the present time. The relative cost of maintaining a rectory may be lower at present than in past years due to fluctuations in the local real estate market. All these things should be reviewed on a regular basis to make sure that the best housing situation for everyone involved can be identified.

BEING REASONABLE AND FLEXIBLE

When a church provides housing for its minister and his or her family, it is best to write out what is expected of the church and what is expected of the family. Both sides must be reasonable and flexible. It may be unrealistic to expect the church community to pay for wall-to-wall carpeting if the wood floors are in good shape. The couple deserves to move into a house or apartment that is clean and in good condition. If children will be living in the house, all safety standards should be met. If pets are involved, a discussion about what is reasonable wear to a home and what constitutes excessive damage is a must. While it may seem too businesslike to create a formal lease, it is best to have the expectations in writing. This gives both the church and the couple a clear understanding of the housing situation and provides the basis for making changes over time. Both sides must be reasonable in their expectations, and everyone should recognize that no house is perfect. A formal lease, or at least a detailed list of expectations and responsibilities, provides a basis for the housing relationship that guarantees that all involved know what is expected of them.

It should not have to be mentioned, but it is vital that the clergy and spouse or partner take responsibility for any damage done to the provided housing. Every house will show signs of wear from the daily activities of its residents, but damage beyond that is not the fault of the house or the church community. There are many examples of excessive damage, but one will suffice. A minister and his partner, with their three children and two dogs, lived in a parsonage for several years. Over the course of their stay, the two dogs ripped out the screening of the porch, scratched deep grooves in its floor, and gnawed through several of the supporting posts. When the family left, the church members found the damaged porch and a house strewn with garbage. All kitchen appliances had to be replaced because they had not been adequately maintained or cleaned. Several doors were off their hinges, and there were two broken windows. The church had not set any guidelines for the upkeep of the house, and did not have any housing agreement in writing. It took several thousand dollars and many months for the church to repair the damage and replace the appliances. Sadly, no amount of money or time could repair the damage done to the relationship between the minister and his former church.

It should likewise not have to be mentioned, but it is vital that the housing provided by the church be in decent and livable condition. The couple should expect to find their new home clean, with appliances that work properly, doors that lock, and windows that have screens. The condition of the house is an indication of the hospitality of the community and should be taken seriously. Again, one example will suffice. One new and newly married pastor and her husband arrived at their manse to find peeling paint and water damage marks on their kitchen ceiling. The other rooms had not been freshly painted and bore the marks of the previous tenants, even though the church had several weeks to prepare the home. When the couple questioned the less than appealing condition of the home, they were told that they were welcome to paint the walls and repair the water damage if they chose—at their own expense. It is no surprise that the minister and her spouse did not stay in that community for very long.

When housing is provided by the church, both the minister and the spouse have an obligation to treat the house and property in a way that shows respect for the community that provides it. If damage is done by a pet, it should be repaired in a timely manner. A yearly walk-through and access for maintenance, with advance notice, are reasonable requests. In other words, the couple should be responsible tenants.

The church that provides a home for the minister must remember that it is private space. When possible, the couple should be allowed to choose the paint colors for the rooms. If the house is on church property, there should be an outdoor area that can be used for the couple's outdoor activities. It is reasonable for the minister and his or her family to have space for a grill, a couple of chairs, and an area for outdoor toys if children are present.

When the couple and the church community show care and respect for the provided housing, positive things happen. One minister and his wife moved into a plain ranch-style parsonage located on the grounds of the church he served. Because there was no place for outdoor activities, the couple asked that a porch be built onto the house rather than have new carpet installed in the house. The church agreed and the porch was built. When it was done, all agreed that it was a great addition. When the next spring arrived, the pastor's spouse created a flower garden around the porch, adding to the beauty of the house and whole property. In the years following, she asked permission to create a second garden—this one on the side of the church itself. The church agreed. This new garden was a gift to the church members who came each Sunday for worship. It was also a gift to future ministers and their spouses because it could be seen from the house's kitchen window. The church and the couple parted on good terms, partly because they showed great respect and consideration for each other through their housing arrangement.

HOUSING AS PUBLIC AND PRIVATE SPACE

For many spouses and their clergy halves, church-provided housing is both public and private. It is borrowed space that will be returned to the church community when the minister leaves. The church must have access to the building to maintain it. This means that there will be church members in the house occasionally, repairing and inspecting its interior and exterior. At the same time, it is space that is a home, not a weekend rental. The couple has every right to create their own private space. Only when they create this space does housing become home. Home creation is not about paint or mortar, but about creating space that nurtures the lives of the people that live there. This process of creating a welcoming and nurturing home within the housing provided by the church can be quite an adventure, with each couple bringing their own unique personalities into their new living space. The couple and the church community can both work together to make this a positive and creative process by keeping a few basic truths in mind:

Everyone Needs a Private Space

The manse is not a truck stop or a diner. Except in emergency situations, church members should not be dropping in at all hours of the day. It is not reasonable to expect the minister and partner to provide entertainment and refreshments after church events. A minister and family have as much right to a private life and free time as anyone else. It is up to the minister, partner, and family to extend invitations to enter into their home; it is not the God-given right of the church members to assume that their presence is always appropriate or welcome.

The House is Not an Extension of the Church Facility

The housing provided for a clergy family should not be considered part of the church's available meeting space. It is not the back-up Sunday school classroom, emergency storage facility, or spare kitchen. If the couple decides to open their home to meetings, that is fine—it is their decision to make. The couple should not feel that the church members expect to use the housing for any church function. They should not be made to feel guilty if they do not want to have church business in their home, regardless of what previous ministers and spouses have allowed.[5]

Everyone Needs Private Time

The minister and his or her partner are entitled to time away from work and should reserve that time without feeling guilty. This time is necessary to nurture family relationships, relax, and connect with people in ways that do not relate to church work. Much of this private time will be spent at home. Whether the housing is on the church grounds or in a nearby neighborhood, it is a private residence—the family resides there and should feel comfortable having a private life within its walls. If the home is always open to church members, the couple loses their private life. This loss is harmful to their relationship, leading to feelings of resentment toward the church community and one another. It is best to avoid this loss of private time by setting good ground rules that work for the current couple, not adopting the rules of former couples.

A necessary step for spouses and their clergy halves is setting parameters for visitors. These parameters will vary from couple to couple. Some couples may maintain an "open door" policy, allowing people into their homes on the spur of the moment. Other couples may decide that their home is not accessible at all to members of the church community, strictly separating their personal time from their community commitments. Most couples will be somewhere in the middle of these positions.[6] These parameters must be set in a way that fosters the lives all involved. The couple should be honest and direct if these parameters are challenged by members of the church, kindly and firmly informing any transgressors that they are not available at present. They may be altered in the future to accommodate the changing needs and interests of the couple—and in light of their experience with a particular community of faith. Relationships take time, energy, and effort. This is true of the pastoral relationship that ministers, and perhaps their spouses or partners, have with the church community. It is equally true of the couple's relationship. Marriages and unions are not fruitful and growing by accident: they are carefully nurtured or they do not grow and remain life-giving. The spiritual, emotional, and physical lives of the couple require time away from the demands of ministry. When this time is respected by the couple, their covenant becomes stronger and each becomes a stronger individual.

Each couple living in provided housing has the right to create a home that ensures private time and personal growth as a couple and as individuals, and that respects the property and members of the church. Having an explicit policy concerning the use of their private space gives the couple and the church community a basis for their relationship outside the job parameters of the minister. The couple sets a good example for others within the community not by allowing their lives to be overtaken by the duties of ministry, but by living together in a way that honors God, the community, and each other.

There are many ways to create a home in church-provided housing that is nurturing for the couple and respectful of the community members. Each couple must work this out with the community and with each other. For example, one couple wrote a letter for the church's monthly newsletter. The letter stated that church members were welcome to stop by within reasonable calling hours (10 A.M.–7 P.M.). If the couple and their children had the time, then visitors would be welcome to stay for a visit. If it was not a good time, visitors would be told this and invited to come again at a better time. In the first few months of their stay, many people did drop by. Some were invited to stay, others invited to come at another time. The couple extended hospitality while fostering their own personal lives by setting explicit parameters that preserved their precious private time. By taking seriously their own need for private space and time while showing care and respect for the community members, the faith lives of all were blessed.

LIVING IN THE COMMUNITY, NOT ON CHURCH PROPERTY

Some churches do not provide a house or apartment, but instead provide a housing allowance. This is a specific amount of money allotted for renting or buying a home within the wider community, and is part of the overall compensation for a minister.[7] As with provided housing, there are advantages and disadvantages to this. The first and most obvious is that the spouse and minister must find their own place to live in a new community, often without any prior knowledge of that area. Members of the church community may provide information about the area, including recommendations for real estate agents; this can make the house hunting process easier.

With a housing allowance, the couple is free to choose a style of house or apartment that is most appealing. The partner and clergy half can decide how close to the church they wish to live. If both are working, they can locate somewhere between the two job sites, making the commute for one or both of them acceptable. If there are children in the family, the location and quality of schools can be considered before buying a home. There are more choices available, and more responsibility for finding the home that best suits the couple.

FINANCIAL REALITIES, HOUSING, AND PEACE

The couple seeking a house within a particular community must take several things into consideration before buying or signing a rental agreement. These are practical considerations that will help the couple decide what they want for their housing and what is possible for them within a particular community.

A couple must base their housing decisions on their financial reality, choosing something they can afford that is suitable for their needs.[8] This may be simple in some communities and quite difficult in others. In one instance, a minister chose to serve a church in a wealthy community on the outskirts of New York City. His total yearly compensation was $3600 short of the actual cost of living in the area, making it necessary for his wife to find employment at the outset of his ministry. The combined income of both was not enough for them to purchase a home, making a rented apartment their only housing option. A couple should determine whether or not they can buy a home in the community without unreasonable debt, or find an acceptable rental property.

Each couple must determine the range of what is acceptable for housing. Rental agents may be helpful in finding a range of housing options, but some guidelines will be required. Some things the couple should determine are:

- The required number of bedrooms and bathrooms
- The outdoor space needed—taking into account pets and children
- Special needs—wheelchair accessibility, one floor only, etc.
- Fixer-upper possibilities—will there be time and energy for this?
- Parking needs, especially in city contexts
- How much money can be spent every month on housing (mortgage, utilities, taxes, etc.)
- Which of these options is acceptable—house, condominium, apartment?
- What a livable commute is for both[9]
- Whether the church requires residency within a certain geographical locale[10]
- If the pastor can live in a neighboring community if necessary or desirable

With these many factors to consider, each couple must determine a range of possibilities that stretch from the ideal to the merely acceptable. If there are many options available, creating a list of acceptable houses from the most to the least favorite is a good way to keep things straight. Each partner may create a list, and then integrate the two into one master list. If a couple cannot agree on a home, temporary arrangements may be considered. Are short-term leases a possibility? Can a couple rent a home with option to buy? Are there suitable seasonal rentals that will allow the couple time to find a home at a leisurely pace?[11] With patience, humor, and time, a couple can find something suitable in which to live and create a home.

TURNING A HOUSE INTO A HOME

A house may be walls and furniture; a home is something else entirely. Once a couple moves into a house or apartment, whether church-owned or not, they begin the job of turning a particular configuration of rooms and outdoor spaces into a home. Assuming that the minimum conditions of cleanliness, safety, and size have been met, the creation of a welcoming private space begins. The physical particulars of this may take a great amount of time and energy, depending upon the family and the space. At this point, the focus is creating a space that nurtures the couple's life, that serves as a place of rest, and that reflects the unique nature of those who live there.

In addition to shelter, a home is an environment that fosters the lives of the people who live within its bounds. Home is a place to relax, to deepen relationships with God and others, to take a break from the world, or to invite the world inside. It is a private place, a place where its residents can be themselves, as individuals and as a family. Within its walls and grounds, the couple lives before God and one with the other. Professional titles and duties are secondary, not the focus of life.[12] Home is the environment for the private lives of the couple and their family. It is a place of creation, respite, activity, dreams, and communal work. If the demands of ministry or other professions dictate the private lives of the family members, adults and children both, then there is no home—just a change of workplace scenery. Home is a place of hospitality, of welcome for all who live there and for those who visit. The following points are signs that a house has been made into a home.

Home Is a Place of Private Time and Space

Are there consistently scheduled private times in the home, times when the couple is unavailable to others except in emergency situations?[13] If no time or space has been clearly separated from the spouse's work and the clergy duties, then it is very difficult to have a home life that is grounded in the covenant promises of the couple's marriage or union. While it is rare that important ministry duties are neglected to foster the life of the couple, it is all too common that the covenant life of the couple is neglected to attend to ministry duties and concerns. If there are no times when a family life is the main focus, especially within living quarters, there is no home, and the lives of all suffer for its lack.

Staying Home for Vacation

If a couple can spend all or part of their vacation time at home, then a private space has been created. There should be no need to leave to guarantee time away from work. Weekly days off and yearly vacation time can be honored without elaborate escape plans and without having to create excuses for not working. Both the partner and the clergy half should feel that time away from ministry and other work is integral to a life lived in relationship, and both should feel no guilt about kindly refusing to allow intrusions into vacations spent at home.[14]

GETTING OUT OF THE DISPLAY CASE

Many couples, especially those who live close to or on church property, feel like their lives are always on display. Some allow the opinions of others to dictate how the house is maintained and what outdoor activities are acceptable. If this feeling of constantly being under observation dictates the private life of the couple, then there is no private home. Only when time at home, both inside and outside the walls, is experienced as private time does the couple have a real home. If the couple has no sense of private space, then the following issues must be addressed:

Are We Being Constantly Watched, or Do We Feel That Way?

If members of the church community are constantly interrupting family time with unannounced visits, then something must be said to the intruders. If members of the community insist on dictating how the private house of the couple is used and maintained, with indirect or direct comments and suggestions, then there is a serious problem. If it is not just a select few that are trespassing by word and deed, then a general announcement kindly insisting on privacy should be made. If the couple cannot enjoy spending time in their own yard without criticism or unwelcome visiting, then the problem is with the expectations of the community.[15]

If the couple assumes that church members are watching and making critical comments when none have been made, then the problem may be one of assumption. If a partner and his or her ministry half maintain a spotless home because they assume it is expected, then they may have internalized a fictitious expectation. If this is the case, then they may be living in light of the supposed opinions of others rather than living in a way that reflects their own needs, dreams, and love. If this is the situation, then they should sit down and decide what level of cleanliness and order is acceptable and able to foster their communal life. House perfection is difficult to achieve and impossible to maintain without spending inordinate amounts of time cleaning and straightening.

Does the Condition of Our House Indicate How We Feel about Ourselves and the Community?

As discussed earlier, each couple must decide how to welcome others into their home and how to maintain their home as a private sanctuary for their communal life. When a home is clean and orderly enough to enhance life, then it nurtures the souls of the family and those who enter as friends and visitors. When a couple is comfortable with their own home's imperfections and their own level of house care, they need make no excuses to themselves or others.

If the two cannot make decisions about their private space with thoughtful intention and kindness, then the condition of their house may reflect their happiness or unhappiness with the church community rather than their own sense of a nurturing private space. If a house is always spotless, then the house is a display window rather than a private space.[16] If the house is consistently dirty and chaotic in appearance, then it may serve as a barrier to keep intruders away—a way of discouraging visitors that does not require a direct addressing of the situation. It may also be a tangible indication of the internal state of those who live there, a way to say "my internal life is in chaos" without using words. If there are serious issues involved, then outside help may be necessary. Cleaning up the house may require more than soap, water, and a broom: it may require exploring psychological difficulties and needs.

Is Our House Ordered for Our Good or to Look Good to Others?

Most couples have some vision of an ideal life, a way of living that seems better than the present reality. When a house is maintained and used based upon a particular look, an idealized look, it does not foster the true lives of those who live within it. A home should maintain a basic standard of cleanliness and order, one that allows the couple and their family and friends to lead interesting lives. A house should not be maintained in a way that denies the lives of the residents in favor of seeming perfect, or at least better. For example, if a couple lives with three kids and a dog, then maintaining a home free of toys and fur is unrealistic. The lawn will not be perfect if it hosts stick throwing and football tossing. If that couple insists on keeping the yard perfect and the house free of toys and hair, then they are fighting their own reality. This does not mean that their floors should be covered in furry dolls and saliva-covered action figures or that their yard should be a minefield of dog poop, but that the standards of cleanliness and order should be reasonable. The couple should live their true lives, not the lives of other people. The very substance of their lives should be personal, reflecting who they are as individuals and as a couple. They are not posing for pictures but living a life.

When a house is created and maintained for the good of those who live there, it reflects their interests and needs. At home, its residents are happy for each other's company. Each person who lives within its walls and yard feels comfortable being who he or she is. This means that the home does not look like one in a magazine or one that is for sale; those houses are for presentation, to appeal not to the people who live there but to those who might want to live there. Perfect homes featured in magazines probably don't look picture perfect every day. They can be great sources of inspiration but should always be adapted to the lives of the ones who live there. What is the point of having a huge kitchen with the latest appliances if no one in the house likes to cook? If reading is a passion for the couple, then bookcases become meaningful and should claim a significant part of the house space. When the art on the refrigerator and the notes on the calendar reflect the lives and interests of the family, the house is ordered for the very substance of their lives. Whether it has the perfect look is immaterial; it should reflect the residents, not the latest trend in home fashion.

If the house does not reflect the lives of those who live there, life becomes inconvenient. The valued activities and objects are not prominent or easily accessible, making those who live there exist as visitors in their own home. While no home can perfectly reflect the lives of its residents, a home planned to be hospitable to those who live there is vital. The home's hospitality can then extend to those who visit, becoming not a perfect house but a space full of kindness and care.

INVITING THE CONGREGATION INTO FAMILY LIFE

When a minister takes a call to a church, he or she agrees to be an integral part of its communal life. As the leader of the church, he or she is invited into the lives of community members, and those members become part of the minister's daily life and work. Because the spouse or partner lives with his or her clergy half, the congregation's members are part of the couple's reality. This is true if the spouse decides to become part of the worship community; it is true to a lesser extent if he or she chooses another faith community. Each couple must decide how to relate to community members in ways that acknowledge their importance and that do not overwhelm the couple's private life. How a couple invites people into their home reflects how they navigate the sometimes choppy waters of privacy and communal participation, between availability and withdrawal, and between enriching the life of the community and nurturing a private life. When making decisions about inviting the community into the home, the spouse and clergy half must be sure to make decisions that reflect care for others and care for themselves, that show hospitality for others and regard for their private life, and that show respect for themselves and others. There is no single or best way to accomplish this, but these final thoughts may be helpful.

Open to Others, Valuing Privacy

The partner and ministering half need and are entitled to privacy. This means that their home and their time should not be available twenty-four hours a day, every day of the week. This kind of openness is expected in a truck stop, not a home. It is exhausting to maintain such openness, and does not set a good example for the church members. Even Jesus withdrew from others when he needed rest and privacy! Unless a couple has greater endurance than Jesus, private time is essential to sanity and a growing faith.

A minister and his or her partner also require a community life. Humans are communal, thriving by interacting with others in meaningful and intentional ways. The communal life of the church should be part of their lives; if the spouse has a different community, then both communities become part of their shared life. Time spent with others, inviting others into the home and visiting the homes of others, can foster the lives of both the minister and the spouse. Each couple must find the balance between availability and absence, one that fosters their lives as individuals and as a couple.[17]

Mutual Respect

The partner, clergy half, and family do not exist for the sole purpose of serving the church. Their lives are not an extension of the church social life, nor is their home the spare kitchen or meeting hall. The members of the community must recognize the autonomy of the couple and respect their right to a private life. Without this respect, the relationship between the minister and the church will be strained, causing damage to the pastoral relationship or to his or her covenant relationship.

The church community does not exist for the sole purpose of serving the minister and his or her family. The community members should be welcoming, but not servile. It is not their job to wait upon the family, nor to supply their every need. The church community existed before extending a call to a particular minister and will continue after he or she has left. There should be mutual respect between the couple and the church, both seeking to enrich the lives and faiths of the other. One does not exist merely to serve the other.

This respect can be obvious or missing from the very beginning of the call. When a parsonage is clean and welcoming, when its walls and grounds are respectfully used, then respect is present. When the church community does not take an interest in helping the couple get settled in their midst, when the couple take advantage of the kindness and helpfulness of the community, respect is absent. A sense of balance and compassion, of hospitality and respect, is crucial for all involved. When these are present, the couple's communal and private lives have room to flourish. Likewise, the life of the community or communities of faith involved is the better because of the couple's presence. All this is reflected in how housing is maintained, made available, and kept private.

Where and how a partner and clergy half live sends a message to their family and friends, to the church community, and to the larger world. When their home provides sanctuary for them, fostering their daily lives by providing a place of retreat and of hospitality, something of the grace of God is visible. Gracious living in this sense is worth far more than the kind found in magazines and on television shows. Living this truth gives a precious gift to the world and immeasurably enriches the lives of all involved.

FIVE

Keeping Sabbath, Keeping Sane

What happens when Sundays, holy days, and holidays are times of intense work rather than days of rest and rejuvenation? As mentioned before, it is one of the ironies of clergy and spouse life that the very events and observances that inspired or deepened a call to ministry become obligatory workdays. Weekly Sabbath becomes working Sabbath; holidays become professional events, involving hours of preparation in addition to the day itself. There are occasional breaks in this, but after accepting a call, both partner and clergy half lose the opportunity to participate in these special days together without leadership roles. Christmas Eve, Christmas, New Year's Eve, New Year's Day, Ash Wednesday, the days of Holy Week, Easter Eve (Vigil), Easter, Pentecost, Memorial Day, Thanksgiving Eve, and Thanksgiving all have their special services; the pastor must plan for these as well as lead the services themselves. Because many of these holidays fall on Sunday only occasionally, the regularly scheduled worship service is usually on its heels. If he or she happens to be part of a multiple staff, perhaps one or two of these require only attendance rather than preparation. Yet for most partners and clergy, Sundays, holy days, and holidays are anything but restful.

For holidays, the busyness for clergy and spouses is twofold: there is the work that goes into the services at church, then the separate family obligations that accompany holidays. Special family gatherings, seasonal events, and all that goes into holiday preparation don't go away or get postponed just because of church duties. What often happens is a "divide and conquer" holiday strategy, with the partner taking on most of the work that falls outside the special services. While this is efficient, it is not ideal. Rest becomes a rare commodity for spouse and clergy half, and spiritual rejuvenation unlikely if the time and work demands become too much. All the church and social obligations may be met, but are they met in a way that leads to a deeper spiritual connection for the couple? Are they met in a way that draws the couple into God's love in new and creative ways? Does the couple find that love for God and neighbor is fostered? If not, then the couple has not had a true holiday. Are there ways to be a couple in covenant relationship, serve God and neighbor, and experience times of rest and reconnection in everyday life?

SABBATH: GOD'S GIFT OF REST AND REJUVENATION

> Observe the Sabbath day and keep it holy, as the LORD your God commanded you. Six days you shall labor and do all your work. But the seventh day is a Sabbath to the LORD your God; you shall not do any work—you, or your son or your daughter, or your male or female slave, or your ox or your donkey, or any of your livestock, or the resident aliens in your towns, so that your male and female slave may rest as well as you. Remember that you were a slave in the land of Egypt, and the LORD your God brought you out from there with a mighty hand and an outstretched arm; therefore the LORD your God commanded you to keep the Sabbath day. (Deut. 5:12–15)

Sabbath is not a day for catching up on sleep and chores that were left undone from the week. It is not a time to get a start on the upcoming workweek. Sabbath is meant to be a time set apart for rest, not just physical rest but emotional and spiritual rest as well. It is a day to reconnect with God and each other. It is not just a time out to catch one's breath after racing through the week's work at light speed.

In the Jewish tradition, all work must be done before the beginning of the Sabbath, leaving the day for God. In Exodus, God instituted the Sabbath, asking the faithful to keep one day apart from the others as a day of rest. Work to sustain life and family is left alone, allowing all people and even animals to enjoy a consistent day free from the constant toil that might separate them from God's presence. There are exceptions to this "no work" rule. In *The Jewish Faith*, Dan Cohn-Sherbok writes: "There are certain situations which take precedence over Sabbath prohibitions . . . instances include circumcision on the Sabbath; dangerous animals may be killed; persons are permitted to fight in self-defense; anything may be done to save a life or assist a woman in childbirth."[1]

The biblical lists of the work prohibited on the Sabbath may seem quite outdated in the modern world, but the principle remains. All people of faith are commanded to keep one day out of seven that is not in service to furthering careers, making money, improving the house, or catching up on studies left undone. The day is kept work free so that the faithful can remember that they are held and nourished by God. This day apart is to remind everyone that living into God's love is not another item on a list of things to do. It is not so much a task as it is a remembrance and an honoring of the correct perspective: that everyone comes from God and will eventually return to God. Building on this foundational truth is difficult at all times, but it becomes close to impossible if no time is set aside for it. The work we do during the six days is necessary for sustaining life and building a peaceful community, but it is not the ultimate reason for existence. Setting a day apart gives everyone a chance to get out of the rat race long enough to realize that God intends life to be much richer than a race to the economic finish line.

In previous years, the larger society might provide a day off for most people. Many states instituted blue laws, prohibiting most businesses from opening on Sundays. In recent years, these laws have disappeared, allowing people to work a second job or get the shopping done on Sunday. It is no longer only health-care, emergency, restaurant, and entertainment staff who work through weekends, but most workers who do not work for a school district, a state, or a federal institution. What used to be culturally mandated—Sundays free from work—may not be an option for most employees. This makes it harder for everyone to enjoy a day of rest.

It would be naïve to think that having blue laws in effect automatically leads to everyone experiencing a day of rest. A day void of shopping and working does not guarantee any spiritual, emotional, or physical rest. Honoring God by observing Sabbath is not an easy or natural thing, and will not occur simply because there is space in the work schedule. Yet, without that time set apart, it becomes even more difficult to observe. A spouse's employment may be contingent on working weekends. Children may have sports team activities that are scheduled for Saturday and Sunday mornings. The time that was open for most people on Sunday is open no longer. To set aside time requires intentionality, and that may limit work availability. A time of rest, a true Sabbath, has always involved sacrifice; in the present time, it is a countercultural move that goes against the notion that all goods and services should be available and accessed at all times. This is true for everyone, and for spouses and partners a difficult truth. Sunday, the nominal day of rest for most Christians, cannot be a Sabbath for the partner and clergy half. There is always work for the minister, often community or professional work for the spouse, and no chance to partake of a full day of rest together. How can a spouse or partner find Sabbath time? What happens when Sabbath is given up to the demands of ministry and other work? Most fundamentally, what is lost when Sabbath disappears?

SABBATH: TIME TO PRAY, TIME TO PLAY

Judaism has consistently maintained the truth that Sabbath rest should be an integral part of the lives of the faithful. How it is observed, and how strictly it is maintained, may vary from one location and time to another. Still, the importance of it remains. But what does Sabbath mean for spouses and partners of pastors who serve Christian churches? While there are many ways to define it, a twofold approach may be helpful: Sabbath is a time to pray and a time to play.

Sabbath is a time to have a conversation with God. Prayer is just that—a conversation. For most people, prayer is a combination of memorized words, grateful thanks, and requests for help. A list of blessings and heartfelt thanks may join those prayers said from memory. A litany of painful circumstances follows—there are always people in dire straits, illness affects all people, and grief over loss is commonplace. Lifting these to God is indeed prayer, perhaps the most familiar kind. Before meals and before sleep are common times for prayer; for some, the day begins in prayer, too. Coming into God's presence to give voice to what is needed and wanted, giving thanks for the gifts received, and lifting other people and situations to God for help are exercises in prayer that take place every day. But is this all there is to it?

Sabbath as a time to pray is about these kinds of prayer, but also about something else. Prayer is not a one-sided affair, but a conversation between God and the person seeking God's presence. Prayer that refreshes and restores involves listening as well as speaking. While few hear the actual voice of God speaking directly to them, there is indeed communication from God. At its most profound, prayer is not about the concerns and joys of life, but about belonging to God; seeking God in prayer is seeking a presence more than an answer. It is seeking the one who created and sustains all of life. In prayer, a person can ask: am I alone? Are my friends and family held in love through all of life's moments? Are we alone and lost in this universe, or do we belong to someone or something greater? Prayer that nourishes is a conversation that addresses these fundamental questions with the positive presence of God. Particular answers may not be found, but a presence is, and that presence provides rest and rejuvenation. Sabbath prayer moves us from communication with God into communion.

This kind of prayer is not something that comes quickly or easily to most adults. It takes time and it takes intention to seek God's presence. God is faithful in being present, but not predictable in what that may mean or look like. Sabbath is a time to pray in this way, giving time, energy, and attention to the conversation. God's presence may be felt without Sabbath rest, but it is less likely to be enjoyed. Prayer as conversation is a bridge to the one who created and loves each individual. Recognizing this, connecting in this way, and living in its light refresh the spirit and restore the soul. Sabbath provides the opportunity to live into this prayer life with intention and hope.

Sabbath is also a time to play. It is a time that is set apart from work that will accomplish specific things, from efforts that further careers or social standing, and from the tasks that must be done to maintain a working household. Play is something done for its own sake, not to accomplish something else.[2] For a couple, Sabbath time set aside for play is the opportunity to reconnect as individuals in relationship rather than as two people fulfilling professional and personal roles. This is time for being together, for enjoying one another's company with no particular agenda. The couple may read, watch movies, play games, or do any number of things enjoyed by both as long as the activities are understood as means to connection rather than as activities that separate. For instance, if a couple happens to enjoy board games, time spent playing cribbage or checkers is a gift of Sabbath rest leading to deeper relationship. On the other hand, a couple that cannot play chess without the loser throwing the pieces at the winner should indulge in other activities that do not pit one against the other. The point is not to win or lose, but to live into the covenant that holds the couple together.

For most adults, setting time apart for play seems wrong somehow. It's as if play is supposed to be left behind with nursery rhymes and stuffed toys. It seems selfish to take energy away from intentional ministry or other tasks. Enjoying the company of the other without accomplishing anything may seem a waste of time. In reality, it is the exact opposite. Relationships take time spent in mutual activities and in mutual rest. What does it accomplish if all the work gets done and the couple loses the ability to enjoy one another? God willing, at some point children will be grown and full time careers set aside. If the couple has lost the ability to enjoy time that is not accomplishing something measurable, what happens to their shared life? Sabbath play is a gift from God that provides the couple with an excuse to enjoy one another's company. Most people commit to each other out of affection—they enjoy each other's company. With the changes that time brings—personal, geographical, work-related—it is critical for the two to remain connected. Play time is for its own sake, for the sake of the two who share in it. Without time set apart from responsibilities, the couple's covenant relationship may be reduced to a functional one. The tasks get done, the careers furthered, and the family grows. What withers is the bond that binds the two together in ways deeper and more mysterious than work or mutual striving for goals can. Sabbath play time brings with it a renewal of spirit and a reconnection that is not reliant on any particular activity or goal. The couple meets again. If there are children, the family play time affirms that they are bound together in love. Delight is the whole point.[3]

Because each couple is unique, play time can take many forms. Games, walks, enjoying scenery, drawing, and enjoying music are just some possibilities. Whatever brings about a lightening of heart and a joy to the spirit will foster play for a couple. The same is true for the larger circle of family and friends: play time together strengthens relationships and affirms love for one another.

It may seem that the play and pray aspects of Sabbath do not fit together well. This is not true. God loves us not for what we do but for who we are. We delight God just by being. Those who play will have a much easier time praying because deep prayer goes beyond asking for help and thanking God for specific things. The words we pray serve as a bridge, leading us to the place where we realize that God awaits us. Play builds a bridge, too, leading us to ourselves and one another. Both are blessings beyond measure because they affirm the fundamental truth that love is about being, not about earning something. Sabbath rest is the foundation for the week because it reveals this truth, allowing the six days of activity to be penultimate rather than the goal of existence. When we grow and put away childish things, as the apostle Paul exhorts, we do not put away play. We put away being childish, making play about winning something or besting someone. Grown-up play is about losing the self in the relationship that connects one to another. There is no point to play other than to be in it with another person, to participate with no thought to its value beyond the moment. In that, the deep truth is seen: we love not because of what do, but because of who we are and who our loved ones are. In that realization is a glimpse of God's love. In that way even the oldest person becomes a child again and is drawn into Christ's kingdom of heaven.

GETTING AWAY FOR THE WEEKEND?

For many people, weekend brings the opportunity for getting away. A couple can get away physically, leaving their hometown to go somewhere else. By getting away, it becomes easier for many couples to leave behind their duties and professional identities. This is an opportunity to spend time together for its own sake. Play is easier when the ever growing laundry piles in the closets and overflowing inboxes on the desks are not in plain view.

The weekend is also a time for visiting family and friends, or inviting them for a visit. This foray into the couple's larger social context can help a couple see their connection to the world beyond their own work and goals.[4] Weekend getaways are an opportunity to experience the playing and praying of Sabbath from a different place and perspective than that of everyday location.

For a clergy partner and the ministering half, weekend getaways are unlikely. Clergy may have three or four Sundays during the year that are free of worship service duties. These are usually taken during vacation time, often all at once rather than sprinkled throughout the year. For the majority of weekends, ministers are preparing for Sunday services, writing and editing sermons, attending special church functions, and taking care of all the things that accompany the worship life of the church. If the spouse's or partner's work does not take up the weekend, then the couple may be able to spend part of Friday and Saturday elsewhere. Once a call to a full-time ministry is taken, weekends away are a rarity for these reasons and a variety of others.

If the spouse does have weekends free from paid employment and faith community obligations, he or she may take a weekend away with little preparation or difficulty.[5] Sabbath time may be set apart as a constant element on weekends, whether spent at home or away. The getting away may not be a geographical one, but a getaway at home that gives an opportunity for playing, praying, resting, and connecting with family and friends. But this Sabbath time must be taken without his or her partner in union, making it unlikely that their covenant relationship will deepen because of it. What can be gained for the spouse or partner is a chance to deepen faith as an individual and as part of the larger family and social context. This does not make it easier to live into a deep covenant relationship directly, because the other half is not participating in the activities and rest. There is no mutuality in the activities, but the time away can be something that nourishes a partner. This may make it possible to bring greater energy and dedication to the union, but it does not bring the same mutual benefits as time together does.

If time set aside on weekends is not possible for a minister and partner, when can a shared Sabbath rest be taken? If the work schedule of the partner leaves some weekdays free, if children or other relatives do not require constant attention and energy from the couple during the week, the couple may choose to take a Sabbath rest on any day of the week. Many clergy take Mondays or Fridays off, making one of these an opportunity for Sabbath rest. Needless to say, there are a lot of "ifs" involved. Any couple who has children in school cannot schedule a family Sabbath on a weekday. When the work schedules of the two do not match up exactly, it becomes difficult to mark off an entire day of shared rest. The time for rest and rejuvenation, the time for prayer and play, becomes fragmented. The couple can choose to take sections of days off together, or they can choose to observe Sabbath apart. No matter what option is taken, fragmentation of time together becomes a fact of life. What can result is a life of treading the spiritual and communal waters. The couple manages to keep above water, avoiding drowning in their work and other commitments, but doesn't really do more than survive. When Saturdays are days of preparation for the clergy half, when family obligations, social commitments or employment claim the partner, it is difficult to keep Sabbath a constant experience in covenant life. Even more troubling, the absence of Sabbath brings with it the forgetting of its true value. The larger society is not going to remind the couple that Sabbath is the day of refreshment, a gift from God. The larger society will reward filling up that time with additional work and goals. It becomes less and less likely that the effort to keep a time apart will be exerted. The tragic truth is that the time apart won't be missed because there is no time apart that allows the couple the opportunity to realize what's missing.

This problem of time is not unique to ministers and spouses. Many couples face the same time bind; many families struggle to take time away from obligations and pursuits. Setting aside a Sabbath day has never been easy or natural. The sacrifices made to maintain a day apart for rest should not be lightly dismissed. The irony for partners and their clergy halves is that the Sabbath rest, not only suggested but commanded for the faithful, is sacrificed to the church's schedule and the needs of the community.

The cost of weekends away, of regular Sabbath, of reconnecting with the covenant partner and extended family, is real. Employment opportunities are lost, advancement of career may be put in jeopardy, and future financial circumstances are affected. The schedule of children's sports and activities changes because availability is not limitless. The values of the family choosing to keep a Sabbath are challenged and sometimes found wanting. What is so valuable about rest, about praying and playing, that it is worth the sacrifice, the inconvenience, and the financial and social costs?

Taking time apart leads to rested lives. Sabbath limits a couple to six days of living life at breakneck speed. The seventh day restores the equilibrium, allowing rest and a chance to reflect on the actions of the week. With time out, a couple may question the pace of life. With prayer and play, the couple has a perspective that is not tied to outward success or financial gain. Weekends away may not be a regular thing for clergy couples, but reserving time out from work, both ordained and lay, should be. Without time out in the couple's routine, vacations become the only time to rest; rather than an opportunity to grow, yearly vacation becomes a chance to recover from the exhaustion of a life lived at top speed. Being overscheduled and overcommitted does not lead to better ministry or better union, because there is no time to focus on what is necessary, what is important, what is desirable, and what is not needed. The spirit of each individual requires time with God and one another to grow in covenant relationship and to grow in service to Christ and the world.[6] This comes with Sabbath play and prayer. This comes with rest. This comes with weekends away.

For the sake of the couple, for the deepening of ministry, for the richness of life lived in relationship with God and others, time away is crucial. Taking that time is not selfish or unreasonable because it leads to a greater sense of connection with God and one another. This refreshes the mind and renews the spirit, which provides a wellspring for the work of all. The costs of keeping a Sabbath, of somehow configuring an occasional weekend away from work, are significant. Reorienting schedules and practices may take a great deal of effort and may not happen immediately. If the spouse or partner is the one who does all the reorienting, if he or she bears the greatest burden in terms of limiting work options, then resentment builds. Both are responsible for the sacrifices necessary for taking Sabbath; both should bear the inconvenience as equally as possible. If arranging the entire schedule around a Sabbath is the task of the partner, it becomes something else to do in an already overbooked life. The anger or irritation that comes from this may make it impossible for the spouse to experience Sabbath as a playful and prayerful time of reconnection.

SETTING ALTERNATIVE HOLIDAYS, CREATING NEW TRADITIONS

The reality of ordained ministry makes it impossible for most ministers and their partners to have a Sunday Sabbath. It also requires working extra hours during holiday seasons and on holidays themselves. The couple does not lose the need for worship and Sabbath when ordained ministry begins: they lose the opportunity to experience them together during the usual times and on the accustomed days. If the covenant partners find their identities in their faith, then the two form a faith community. Family is the first faith community for most people, beginning in their childhood homes. This continues throughout life, although not much thought may be given to its importance. For a minister, partner, and any children they may have, the faith community of family may become the context for alternatives to the Sunday and holiday work and worship bind. This does not mean that the larger faith community or communities are not necessary for the couple to live out their lives of faith, but the family faith community can be a source of nourishment when the demands of ministry and other work make it impossible for the couple to worship together.[7]

When every holiday requires the minister to prepare and lead worship services for the church, a couple may choose to set alternate holidays. These do not take the place of Easter services or midnight Christmas Eve gatherings, but they can provide the partner and clergy half the opportunity to be together in prayer and observance of faith. They should be sources of nourishment, not additional duties that increase holiday exhaustion. In other words, they should be simple, requiring no great attention to detail and costing little if anything. They are not productions, but instead quiet spaces for the couple to come together before God to acknowledge and celebrate the holy days.

There are many ways for a covenant couple to celebrate the holidays that must be working days. The couple can decide on alternative holidays. The couple can limit the busyness of holidays and holiday seasons by centering their time and energy on those activities that are necessary and that are meaningful. Sitting down together to discuss and plan holiday seasons, taking time to schedule holiday rest, and keeping one another from working into exhaustion are all good ways to lower the stress that comes from overcrowded schedules and overcommitted personal calendars. Each couple is different, so there is no single way to celebrate together. The following suggestions are merely that—suggestions. They may be suitable to some, and may provide a jumping off point for others to create their own ways of celebrating holidays.

Day after Celebrations

The day after a major holiday is often a day when offices are closed and few meetings are held, making it a good day to reserve for the spouse and clergy half to have their own holiday rest. The day after Christmas can be spent together, either with the larger circle of family and friends or without them. In any case, the day can be one of rest, with play and prayer at its heart. A post-Thanksgiving holiday has an added bonus of avoiding the massive crowds rushing to purchase gifts of all kinds. The couple is free to choose how their day-old holiday will be spent, which is a profound gift in itself.

Soon after Celebrations

For many married couples, holidays mean choosing one side of the family over the other. One side is visited on Christmas, the other for Easter; Mother's Day is spent one place, Thanksgiving another. Unless the families involved are on friendly terms and located in the same area, choices are made. With a minister and partner, holidays are often spent without extended family. This is especially true if the couple does not live near one family or the other. It is exhausting to attempt leading services, preparing for holidays, and traveling considerable distances.[8] One option that allows the couple to be with their extended families is to have a "soon after" celebration. The couple and larger family set a date within a couple of weeks of a major holiday to have their own celebratory get-together. The advantages to this are many: the spouse and minister have time to rest after the extra work that holidays bring, the time with extended family is centered upon the family rather than expected holiday activities, everyone enjoys a special day when the post-holiday doldrums set in, and everyone has the opportunity to relax. It takes some planning to pull this off, but it is well worth the effort.

A couple may choose to have "soon after" celebrations without the extended family. This can be a wonderful getaway opportunity for the two of them, or for the two and any children they may have. This celebration is a spiritual health day, one that fosters the covenant promises of the couple and reaffirms their commitment to God, each other, and their family. It is a time to reflect upon the holiday that has just passed, and ponder what the future holds. Prayer and play combine to refresh the couple after their busy holiday activities, both sacred and secular.

Lesser Feasts and Fasts

For those who find their faith communities within liturgically centered traditions, the Eastern Orthodox churches and the Anglican Communion among others, the schedule of saints' days are readily available. For those in other traditions, a brief time on the Internet will result in finding a calendar of saints. A couple may choose to have a holiday on one or more of the days dedicated to the saints whose lives are noted and celebrated every year on specific days. The feast of St. Joseph might be a good time to celebrate God's gracious presence with humanity. Any one of the disciples' days can be the focus for a time of prayerful and playful thanks for the life of Christ. There are myriad possibilities to be found in the calendar of saints, making a true holy day that allows the spouse and clergy half a chance to experience a holiday that revives the mind, body, and spirit. It is also a good way to learn more about the many faithful who stand among the communion of believers—a communion that includes the couple, the faithful who have died, and the faithful who live in this time.

Sabbath Days

Very few couples celebrate a Sabbath day of rest every week, even though it comes from the wisdom of God. Taking twenty-four hours away from work and other obligations seems an impossible goal for most people, whether involved in ordained ministry indirectly, directly, or not at all. But the profound rest and nourishment that comes from Sabbath feeds the body, mind, heart, and soul in ways that nothing else can. Sabbath reorients lives, moving the overbooked work schedule into the larger context of God's creative purposes. It is a gift that blesses the couple, their family and friends, and the community or communities of faith that they serve.

The life pace that most people live, regardless of profession, is hectic to the point of insanity. There is little if any time free from work, school, cleaning and upkeep, and extracurricular activities. Busy, busy, busy is everyone. How can Sabbath be adjusted to fit into such schedules? Some have suggested "Sabbath moments," odd times during traffic jams and in grocery store check-out lines that can be opportunities to focus on God. Lunchtime meditations, prebreakfast prayers, and thanksgiving during morning showers can add a bit of holiness to the days lived in the fast lane. Other suggestions include the odd weekend away, perhaps during the free Sundays of vacation. Quiet days during the week, led by someone else, can bring peace to the turmoil of life. But these things, while good in themselves, are not enough. The truth is that Sabbath cannot be adjusted to fit into the modern schedule: just as in ancient times, the modern schedule must be adjusted to Sabbath. It is a question of which reality is larger—God's nourishing weekly gift or the daily grind blessed by society? For a partner and clergy half, there is no easy way to experience Sabbath. Depending upon their financial situation, there may be no way to have a weekly Sabbath and pay the bills. What results is a life without Sabbath, and often without the expectation of ever having regular Sabbath time. Sometimes it is only when the body or heart give out that Sabbath is seen for the necessity that it is.

In the best of all worlds, the covenant couple will schedule Sabbath before they reach the point of exhaustion—before the call to ordained ministry is pitted against their continuing in relationship. The following imperfect possibilities may help.

From Sundown to Sundown

The traditional Jewish Sabbath begins at Friday at sundown and ends Saturday at sundown, allowing the couple to prepare for its beginning during the day and to prepare to reenter the working life during the evening of its ending. For the couple without children in school, it is possible to have Sabbath from any weeknight into the next weeknight. This allows for some flexibility for two work schedules. Thursday night through Friday night is often a good option if the spouse's work does not include all weekdays.[9] If it does, then the traditional Friday night to Saturday Sabbath may be possible. The clergy half would have to prepare for worship by writing sermons before Friday night, but would have Saturday evening to finish up whatever work did not get done. On the Fridays and Saturdays that include weddings or other special events, the couple may move the Sabbath to another day or take their Sabbath time apart. This is not a perfect situation, but better than no regular Sabbath.

From Sunrise to Sunset

If a covenant couple cannot alter schedules to have a full twenty-four-hour time of rest, then a day of rest from first light to the coming of night may be a good option. This can be on the minister's day off if the spouse's work schedule allows, and if it can be cleared of any extracurricular activities that the children of the family may have. This day can be during the week or on Saturday. If there are things that cannot wait until the next day, the couple can choose to do them before sunrise or in the evening. The full day of rest will vary in length, according to the season. Winter Sabbaths will be shorter while summer ones will be longer. In any season, the day set apart will be long enough to require planning. It will also be long enough to allow the couple to reconnect and share their playing and praying.

Separate Sabbaths

If financial necessity, incompatible work schedules, or children's activities make it impossible for the couple to take a Sabbath time together, the two could choose to celebrate Sabbath separately. The minister may choose to keep a Sabbath day during the week, on his or her day off. This allows for a time of rest and reflection that can help nourish the spirit and feed the soul.

The partner or spouse may choose to take Saturday or Sunday for a Sabbath day, especially if work commitments keep him or her busy during the weekdays. While the clergy half prepares sermons, attends functions, and generally considers the weekend days full workdays, the partner can let go of work and household obligations. If there are children, they may participate in this Sabbath as well. By having a separate Sabbath, the spouse can keep a time apart, attending to the needs of the soul that are met through play and prayer. This separate Sabbath may not directly improve the covenant relationship, but can strengthen the partner as an individual. This can bring energy into the relationship that would be missing altogether if no Sabbath at all were experienced.

Taking the time to plan for and participate in Sabbath every week is difficult for everyone, not just ministers and their spouses. Some may feel selfish in demanding such time away from meaningful work. Others may feel that the planning necessary to keep the day free is too difficult; it may seem easier to work all seven days rather than overload six with work. It is up to every couple to decide the worth of Sabbath for them. Being still, being present to God and others, and believing in the value of play may not seem valuable in the face of all that must be accomplished to pay bills, advance in professions, and foster children's social and academic futures. The worship community itself may look askance at such a seemingly frivolous waste of work time. When Sabbath is sacrificed through necessity or choice, something holy and enjoyable moves out of reach. The two who promised to work out their relationship in the context of their faith, and their faith in the context of their covenant, lose the opportunity to keep those promises on their weekly calendar. Other opportunities will arise, and the union may grow without Sabbath. But the couple is settling for less than is offered in a life lived in faith and in relationship. It is a shame to settle for scraps of time when a banquet of opportunity awaits with every Sabbath.

BLESSING AND DANGER: BECOMING PROFESSIONALLY RELIGIOUS

One of the great blessings of ordained ministry is the daily encounter with the sacred in life. Ministers take part in the lives of the faithful during their darkest and brightest hours. Truths are told and heard that quicken the heart and foster compassion. The beauty of the worship service is experienced as a leader and prime participant. The minister presides over weddings and funerals, baptisms and confirmations, and the weekly gift of communal worship.

Yet, one of the *greatest* dangers of ordained ministry is the daily encounter with the sacred in life. Ministers take part in the lives of the faithful during their darkest and brightest hours. Difficult truths are told and heard that weigh heavily on the heart and spirit. The beauty of the worship service is unavailable except as a prime participant. A minister presides over weddings and funeral, baptisms and confirmations, and the weekly communal worship as a professional always; gone are the days of showing up to church and experiencing the grace of someone else's leadership, someone else's insight, someone else's sermon. The constant contact with profound events can exact a terrible toll on a minister, leaving him or her drained beyond the usual weariness that accompanies a busy schedule. If things become too overwhelming, the pastor may create a protective shell around his battered spirit or her bruised heart. This allows continued functioning and gives the pastor a distancing space that spares him or her from drowning in depths of sadness over the state of the world. Most ministers understand why Jesus wept when he saw Jerusalem: even without an impending crucifixion, the needs of God's people are beyond measure. Perhaps this is why Jesus often retreated for prayer.

If a true rejuvenating Sabbath is not part of a minister's ongoing ministry and life, then he or she may become a purveyor of sacred objects rather than a follower of Christ living out a vital, breathing, sustaining faith. The pastor may feel like he or she is creating a religious façade, an outer appearance of a deeply nourishing relationship with God in the Spirit. God willing, the community members still find their lives drawn more deeply into God's life through their pastor's work, but the pastor may be in danger of a burnout of the most profound nature. What happens when the burden of ministry becomes too great for one person to bear? What happens when ministry does not lead to abundant grace and overarching peace? In the end, a life lived behind a façade of joy leads to a limited ministry and a truncated spiritual life.

When a spouse or partner is living through this, things become quite complicated. Many try to lessen the burdens of their ministering half by taking on some of the ministry duties within the faith community or by attending the majority of events and services at the church. Others choose to leave the explicit ministry to their other half, but assume the majority of the work necessary for keeping a home and family intact. The partner manages the context of the covenant relationship, keeping the home fires burning. Personal issues and needs may be put off or completely ignored because they seem so minor in the face of all the sadness in the world. This may be done with a smile firmly pasted on the face, all in the effort to provide the faith community with a strong leader and a deepening spiritual life. The façade that is presented as a survival tactic may be created for two rather than just the one who is ordained. When this happens, the couple becomes professionally religious rather than professing the faith. If this situation is not addressed and corrected, it can lead to profound exhaustion and an exit from ordained ministry or happy marriage.

Fortunately, spirit-numbing exhaustion is not the inevitable outcome for either the spouse or the ordained half. A deeper well of strength can be tapped for both, one that gives the soul nourishment in trying times. Strength is drawn from this well when some basic truths are admitted and treasured by both. It involves a profound change in perspective that frees them from the burdens they cannot and should not shoulder while providing energy to do those things that are theirs to do.

No One Must Drag God into Difficult Situations

God is already in the midst of the worst events and times of suffering. A minister, ordained or lay, must recognize that he or she is not responsible for bringing God into the world. He or she affirms the presence of God rather than trying to produce the Holy Spirit on demand. A pastor is a faithful witness to Christ's presence in the world—which is quite enough. It is not necessary or possible for anyone to create the Holy, and anyone who tries will tire quickly and needlessly. No one is called to be a miracle worker, or sustain faith and hope single-handedly. No one is without the presence of the Holy Spirit in any ministry, no matter how significant or mundane.

For the partner or spouse, knowing that God is already present in difficult circumstances can be a great relief. God's presence may not be felt in a way that is obvious or immediately comforting, but no one is alone in his or her struggles. God is big enough to accept complaints about the price paid for union with a pastor, including any colorful language deemed necessary.

No One Person's Work Is Indispensable

Each person is unique and cannot be replaced by another person. At the same time, no one person's work is so crucial that the worship community will collapse without it. Each ministry is unique and valuable, but no one minister controls the fate of the faith. All people of Christian faith are called to use their gifts to serve God and the world. If the ordained minister is trying to do all the ministries of the community, he or she is bound to fail through exhaustion. More important, he or she denies others the opportunity to work out their baptismal calls to ministry. Everyone offers unique gifts and abilities, gifts from God for service to others. No person can be replaced, but more than one individual is capable of fostering the life of the church.

If a pastor serves the faith community in a way that makes that community reliant on him or her alone, damage is done to all concerned. The community begins to see itself and its work only as the extension of the minister's work and vision rather than as God's presence for the world. This results in a weakened community and an exhausted minister.

For the spouse, knowing that the future of the faith does not rest solely on the shoulders of his or her clergy half means questions about the cost of ministry can be raised. Keeping silent as the minister works toward exhaustion and an early grave is not loyalty to the faith and is not necessary. The spouse may be the only person who can address the consequences of ministry. The cost of ordained ministry is paid by the couple, not just the individual. Knowing that the Christian faith in general and the community in particular will not collapse without the overworking of the pastor brings perspective to conversations about the wisdom of workaholism.

Grace Is Present

No matter how a covenant couple has configured their work and personal lives, change is possible. The covenant union is meant for the uplifting of both, not for the frustration of both. While living out a covenant relationship in light of ministry and living out a ministry in the context of a covenant relationship can be difficult, the couple should seek the grace that comes with such difficulty. What grace comes from the burdens of ordained ministry and the work of the spouse? How does this very complexity lead to a deeper understanding and appreciation of life? Where is the blessing in it all? Both the partner and the clergy half should ask themselves these questions—and listen to the answers together. Overcoming difficulties together can bind the couple more closely even as facing them alone can divide them permanently.

Sanity and Sabbath go together, keeping the couple aware of the grace of God in their midst. Whenever the two are together, Christ is present. This is not always felt but it remains true. Taking Sabbath can help a couple experience this truth, putting their lives in the context of God's love that nourishes and sustains them in the complex context of covenant and ordained ministry.

DREAMING DREAMS: THE SABBATH OF RETIREMENT

> Then afterward I will pour out my spirit on all flesh;
> your sons and daughters shall prophesy,
> your old . . . shall dream dreams,
> and your young . . . shall see visions. (Joel 2:28)

At some point, working as a full-time minister is no longer wise or possible. Many denominations have a mandatory retirement age that quietly but firmly insists that the ongoing work of the church is handed over to newer and younger ministers. This does not mean that a pastor is forced to quit working altogether, but it does mean that the running of the communal life is handed on to someone else.[10] Retirement is the opportunity to let go of the day-to-day duties that demanded so much time and effort in favor of taking up the task of dreaming dreams. This is true for both men and women in their retirement years (regardless of Joel's gender exclusive language in the original text). But what does it mean to dream dreams?

Dreams seem rather insubstantial and unimportant to most people. Perhaps they reveal truths about the individual's personality but are not really helpful in getting along in the world. Dreamers do not feel obligated to act on their dreams for financial gain or the betterment of society in all situations. Dreamers dream because the dreams themselves enrich the world by pointing people of all ages to the mysterious nature of reality. Dreamers are not fooled by the commonplace appearances of everyday objects and events, for they see through these into the sanctity of everyday life. Dreaming dreams of faith, dreams of God, is nothing more or less than seeking to see the fingerprint of God in the heavens and the footprints of Christ on the earth. Retirement that brings freedom from full-time duties brings the opportunity to dream dreams, to see God in everything, every person, and every moment. These visions are usually the gift of childhood and of old age because those who live in between are too busy to wait for them. The young know that dreams come without intentional work; they tell the world about their dreams in simple words and colored pictures. The old regain entry to this childlike dream life when they let go of their professional and work identities and expectations; they reveal their dreams of faith in poetic words that entrance the spirit rather than argue a point. It is the wondrous gift of retirement that makes it possible, perhaps even enviable, to give over the reins of societal position and power to the younger generation.

For an ordained minister facing the end of his or her full-time ministry, retirement may well seem like death. Like all people, ministers often confuse their work with their worth, making retirement the doorway to worthlessness. Rather than dream the dreams of God, old age leads to depression and an annihilation of the self that is a foreshadowing of physical death. For some, this leads to a premature death: what is left to live for when the work of a lifetime is taken away?

For the partner or spouse, the clergy half's retirement offers something sacrificed for the many years of full-time ministry: the opportunity to worship together, to hear and discuss sermons and services as community members only, and to take Sabbath and holidays in any number of lengths, ways, and locations. The work lives of both can be set aside and both can take up the new work of dreaming dreams. Their relationship is for its own sake, not to create and sustain a vibrant leadership. Children are grown or nearly grown, making available time and energy long claimed by others. Why not dream the dreams, why not pray for visions of God's graceful presence, why not seek to see in every person, place, time, and thing the possibility of God's revelation? Most of all, why not do these things with the one who has been a covenant partner all along?

For some couples, retirement for one or both of the partners is not possible at the same time. One or both may choose to keep involved in the leadership of specific ministries or part-time work. Eventually, physical limitations will urge the couple to slow their pace and look for the gifts of age rather than carping on what has been lost. Sabbath may become, for the first time, the center of the couple's schedule. Prayer and play become their primary tasks and their most profound joy rather than occasional treats. Neither requires great physical strength, and some forms of both are possible and gratifying even with slower reflexes and thought processes. Neither requires professional credentials, just an open heart and a listening spirit. The dreams of one are no more valuable than the dreams of the other; shared, those dreams weave a bond of great worth, for it connects them to God and each other ever more deeply.

There are some profound changes that take place as age advances, including the breakdown of the physical and sometimes mental abilities taken for granted for so many years. But it is foolhardy to lose the gift of dreaming dreams in the inevitable degeneration of the body. The time of dreaming dreams has its own wonder and power, and the couple who accepts its gifts may live into a Sabbath rest more profound and true than any they have experienced since infancy. Dream the dreams together when possible, for that is the gift of Sabbath after the years of time-consuming ministry.

SIX

What Every Couple Should Know

A central task for any couple, clergy or otherwise, is how to preserve and nurture their emotional bond over time. As any couples' therapist knows, it is evident that promoting partners' emotional connection is frequently as challenging as it is important to their overall quality of life. This chapter was approached with the following question in mind: Given only one chapter in which to convey what every clergy couple should know, what would that chapter include?

First and foremost, couples need to know that there are very specific, practical, and concrete steps they can take to protect and enhance their relationships, and that these steps were derived from years of rigorous scientific investigation. Consequently, the main purpose of this chapter is to provide a brief overview of what seminal research tells us contributes to marital quality and distress. The goal of this chapter is to cue readers to both warning signs and strengths so they can begin inventorying their own relationships and exploring the implications of the research for the unique realities of clergy relationships. And because it is a topic that couples frequently raise as a major concern, some thoughts are included on the role of communication in shaping the quality of intimate relationships. Finally, some advice is provided to consumers who are seeking couples therapy. Although many of the themes touched upon in this chapter are discussed throughout the book in different language, the emphasis of this chapter is providing a clinical and research perspective on these themes so readers can identify for themselves the most salient areas of overlap between the spiritual and the clinical.

WHAT MAKES MARRIAGE SUCCEED OR FAIL

Researchers and therapists have studied marriage and intimate relationships closely and, through a body of research spanning decades, have identified the factors contributing to marital discord and dissolution, as well as the factors contributing to marital satisfaction and long-term relationship stability. One of the most important figures in helping us understand marriage is John Gottman, Ph.D. Dr. Gottman is a psychologist at the University of Washington who has spent more than thirty years studying marriage. Through his rigorous and innovative research, Gottman has identified the crucial risk and protective factors differentiating satisfying, durable marriages from those at risk of discord and dissolution. These factors are very specific behavioral, emotional, cognitive, and physiological patterns, and they are such powerful determinants of marital quality that Gottman has been able to predict whether a marriage will fail or succeed with around 90 percent accuracy. The upshot of Gottman's research is this: How well a couple manages conflict and, more importantly, how well a couple connects during nonconflict times determine to a large degree whether the marriage will succeed or fail. To be sure, Gottman's risk and protective factors do not comprise the whole picture of marriage, but they do provide a scientifically supported starting point to help us inventory marital strengths and vulnerabilities.

RISK FACTORS: WHEN CONFLICT ERODES CLOSENESS

Common sense tells us that too much fighting is likely to be bad for marriage. Reduce the conflict and enhance the long-term chances of success. What Gottman discovered was that it's not so much the presence, frequency, or intensity of conflict that shapes marital quality but how effective a couple is at preventing it from becoming personal and eroding their emotional attachment during nonconflict times. The importance of Gottman's work is that he identified the specific behavioral, emotional, and physiological components that differentiate healthy conflict from conflict that damages relational bonds. What follows is a very brief introduction to his work that is simply intended to sensitize readers to important risk and protective factors. References to Gottman's original work are provided at the end of the book, and readers are encouraged to seek this out for a more comprehensive understanding of the material.

Gottman studied couples in great detail in his "Love Lab" at the University of Washington. Mimicking an apartment, this lab was a naturalistic setting in which he could observe, measure, and record the minute details of couples' day-to-day interactions. He observed how they cooperated on tasks, discussed problems, argued, expressed affection, made up, and so on. He even measured heart rates and drew blood to understand their physiological responses in key marital interactions. He followed couples over years and identified six very specific warning signs that helped him predict emotional detachment and divorce, and seven specific protective factors that were common to satisfying, durable relationships. Keep in mind as you read the following that these factors are so important to shaping marital quality that, knowing them, Gottman has been able to predict whether a couple would divorce with over 90 percent accuracy. It is also important to remember that each of the risk factors is grounded in partners' misguided, counterproductive efforts to influence one another to get their needs met in the relationship. These underlying needs are legitimate, as are the attempts to influence. Only the tactics are not, and, as we'll see later, there are ways that partners influence that are predictive of relationship resiliency and satisfaction.

Warning Sign One: A Harsh Startup

Problems and conflict are inherent in relationships, and even the best of marriages are no exception. How a discussion about a problem or conflict starts is vitally important, however. If a couple begins discussing a problem and it starts negatively, it will almost always end negatively, according to Gottman's research. A harsh startup occurs when a discussion starts with a critical, sarcastic, or contemptuous tone. In fact, he claims that he can tell with 96 percent accuracy the outcome of a fifteen-minute conversation by observing only the first three minutes. A harsh startup essentially destroys any chance for a successful resolution to a problem because it virtually eliminates any chance a spouse has of enlisting his or her partner's cooperation.

Some examples might include: "I guess it didn't occur to you that someone else might have needed the car today?" "Thanks so much for leaving your shit all around the house for me to pick up when I got home from work." "You're not exactly Warren Buffet when it comes to finances, now, are you?" To be sure, there were legitimate complaints underneath each of these opening salvos, but they never got taken seriously because the partner was focused on responding to the verbal artillery shells.

Warning Sign Two: The Four Horsemen of the Marital Apocalypse

Please commit the following four words to memory: Criticism. Contempt. Defensiveness. Stonewalling. Gottman calls these the Four Horsemen of the Marital Apocalypse because they are so damaging to a couple's emotional bond that their appearance often heralds the end of the relationship.

The first Horseman, criticism, occurs when a partner takes a legitimate grievance and turns it into a personal attack. The criticizing partner turns the "offending" partner's behavior into evidence of a deficient personality or faulty character. Forgetting to put out the trash becomes a reflection of laziness. Not pulling over immediately when the "check engine" light comes on is symbolic of daftness. Sometimes a criticism can follow on the heels of what initially appears to be a compliment. For example, "Thanks for dropping the kids off at daycare this morning. Now imagine doing that every day like you said you would when you first got laid off." Keep in mind that a criticism is qualitatively different than a complaint. A complaint is focused on a specific behavior: "I'm upset that you didn't get the school supplies for the kids like we agreed. It's going to be really inconvenient for me to go after work." A criticism is personal and often makes a global statement about the other's character: "I don't know why I asked you in the first place. You always find some excuse." (Note that criticisms often contain "you always" and "you never.") Similarly, criticisms are sometimes couched as accusations that one spouse doesn't love or prioritize the other: "Am I even on your radar screen? You can remember every score from every football game ever played but you can't remember one simple thing I ask you to do."

Contempt, the second Horseman, goes beyond criticism to express disgust or disdain. Contempt is often an expression of pent-up hostility that may stem from months or years of unresolved problems and disappointments festering beneath the surface. It can be conveyed through a patronizing tone, a roll of the eyes, a disgusted sigh or condescending facial expression. Spouses may express contempt through name calling, mockery, or sarcasm. Sarcasm is perhaps the most common expression of contempt seen by therapists working with distressed couples. Many clients express pride in their sarcastic wit and ability to verbally one-up their partner. When asked what they most want from their spouses, such clients' answers may range from "I want more help with the kids" to "I want to know she still loves me." When asked if sarcasm ever gets them what they want, the answer invariably is "no."

As harsh startups, criticisms, and expressions of contempt increase, people will naturally start to react defensively. Defensiveness, the third Horseman, is more, however, than simply an innocuous attempt at self-preservation. Gottman argues that defensiveness is damaging because it is really more of an effort to reverse the blame, which thwarts partners' capacities to be open to and to accept influence from one another. Defensiveness ultimately ends up escalating the conflict as partners increasingly justify their positions and refuse to truly acknowledge the validity of the other's concern. The defensive partner often defines him- or herself as a victim simply responding reasonably to the egregious behavior of the other. It can take many forms but we all know defensiveness when we hear it. "Yes—but" is a frequently a sign of defensiveness, as in "Yes, I may have overreacted. But the only reason I yell at the kids so much is because you let them get away with murder." Notice that this maneuver essentially invalidates the original concern or criticism (yelling at the kids) and fires back with its own (insufficient discipline). Any opportunity to resolve the original issue is lost in the ensuing back-and-forth of justifications and counter charges. To be sure, the original issue is likely to be couched in criticism or contempt, but choosing to react without defensiveness may de-escalate an already heated argument.

Stonewalling is usually the last of the Four Horseman to appear. Stonewalling happens after months or years of harsh startups, criticisms, and expressions of contempt have poisoned the overall relationship atmosphere with negativity. The stonewalling partner, discouraged that there will ever be any satisfactory resolution to the conflict, simply withdraws in an attempt to avoid escalating it further. Initially the withdrawal may be from conflict interactions, but eventually it becomes a withdrawal from the relationship as a whole. As one partner withdraws (Gottman's research tells us it is the husband who withdraws 85 percent of the time), the other intensifies the negativity in an attempt to engage the withdrawer. In response, the withdrawing partner disengages further, and so on. Stonewalling is evident in a variety of behaviors, including poor eye contact, a bored or annoyed facial expression, "yes dear," "whatever you say dear," monosyllabic responses, and even physically leaving the scene. A withdrawing partner conveys the sense that he or she doesn't care about the concerns of the partner, but this posture usually emerges after negativity has become pervasive in the relationship and some degree of hopelessness has set in.

Marital therapists have variously called the interaction pattern characteristic of the Four Horsemen the pursue-distance, pursue-withdraw, or approach-avoid pattern (and in the early, politically incorrect years of marital therapy, was sometimes referred to as the nag-withdraw pattern). In the context of heterosexual marriage, the archetype of this dynamic is a "pursuing" wife and "withdrawing" husband. Martin and Elena, for example, came to therapy because they could not discuss even minor day-to-day challenges without it turning into a barrage of character attacks. In their first session, they were asked to describe a common problem situation in their marriage. They began describing an argument they had the previous month about Martin going hunting with friends instead of going to a doctor's appointment with Elena during which she was to have a mass on her shoulder biopsied. After a matter of seconds, however, they lost the ability to tell me about the previous argument and actually fell back into the argument itself.

Elena: "This is so typical. It never entered your mind that I might've wanted you to be at the appointment? I was scared to death!"

Martin: "You never told me you wanted me to go! I told you two days before I was going hunting that day. Why didn't you tell me then that you wanted me there? I had the day off. I could have gone."

Elena: "I told you I was worried! Anyone with half a brain would have put two-and-two together. Anyone who gave a damn, anyway . . ."

Martin: "This is pointless." (Looks to the therapist) "There's no winning with her. I never get it right." (Sighs, slumps in his chair.)

With this couple, the pattern had become an automatic response by the time they sought therapy. It could be triggered talking about work, the kids, the pets, holiday plans, or even the laundry. Everyday problems or misunderstandings that the couple managed well earlier in their relationship somehow got transformed into personal attacks and thoughts (and threats) of divorce. Like most couples caught up in the pursue-distance pattern, their arguments had a disturbingly familiar "here we go again" feel to them and had been going on for months or years before they decided to come to therapy. The particular issues about which they were arguing rarely got resolved and they were both left feeling hurt, traumatized, distant, and discouraged. Over time, the pursue-distance interaction pattern may erode the emotional bond necessary to a resilient, satisfying relationship.

Spouses may become more and more emotionally detached from one another, they may begin living separate lives in the same home, and the relationship may ultimately dissolve. It is important to note here that Gottman's work tells us that often the primary threat to a marriage isn't single or dramatic instances of poor judgment or breaches of trust. Rather, the damage is caused by a prolonged atrophying of marriage's emotional connective tissue through months and years of the pursue-distance pattern and the Four Horsemen. The presence of one or two Horsemen or some degree of pursue-distance does not spell marital doom, but as these factors increase in a relationship, the more at-risk that relationship is for emotional detachment and dissolution.

Warning Signs Three and Four: Flooding and Physiological Arousal

Flooding occurs when one is so inundated by the negativity of the partner that he or she simply shuts down in an attempt to avoid further damage. The marital terrain feels like a minefield and any misstep is likely to result in an explosion of criticism or contempt. According to Gottman, a flooded partner is likely to become hypervigilant in an attempt to avoid setting off the marital landmines. Clients often liken this to the proverbial "walking on egg shells" feeling.

Flooding is accompanied by physiological arousal, such as increased heart rate, elevated blood pressure, and the secretion of adrenaline, characteristic of a fight-or-flight state. This means that during intense conflict, spouses are likely to be operating on the basis of their most primitive instincts rather than on the basis of any intellectual decision-making process or deeply held principles. Many people have had the experience of thinking of the perfect rejoinder minutes after they walk away from an argument. Similarly, people who have experienced test anxiety understand the frustration of knowing the material inside and out but being unable to recall it during the actual exam. These phenomena occur in part because we lose access to the range of our own complexity when we're under stress.

Men, as it turns out, are more physiologically vulnerable to this than women in the midst of conflict. When confronted, women can self-soothe in a matter of minutes, whereas men can simmer for several hours before being able to calm down. A man's physiological arousal can be dissipated quickly through retaliation, however. Ever hear of two men, friends even, stepping outside to "work it out?" Within minutes, they can have their issue put to rest and their friendship back on track. Yes, this is primitive, but that's the central point: A man in a conflict with his wife may be confronted with the most primitive of choices. He can retaliate (that is, fight) with criticism or contempt, escalating the argument and damaging the relationship further, or withdraw (flee) in an attempt to prevent adding more fuel to the fire. But this is often a lose-lose situation for the couple because flight looks to his partner like the man doesn't care, possibly resulting in more criticism and more escalation. To the man, however, withdrawal may look like the lesser of two evils because at least he is not pursuing retaliation as his instincts may be pushing him to do. Gottman argues that these physiological differences between men and women mean that women, being more physiologically able to cope with conflict, are more likely to bring up relationship problems. Men, on the other hand, are more physiologically vulnerable to fight-or-flight responses, and consequently are more likely to avoid talking about such concerns.

Warning Sign Five: Failed Repair Attempts

Because conflict is a factor in any marriage, how couples protect their connection during conflict is critically important to the overall well-being of the relationship. Couples who do well in the long term are effective at repairing their bond during conflicts to prevent them from getting out of control. Gottman's work tells us that repair attempts can take a variety of forms, ranging from humor in the midst of an argument to statements such as "This is getting too serious. Let's try again tomorrow." If these repair attempts are consistently offered and accepted, the relationship can withstand even the

Four Horsemen, according to Gottman. If they are not offered, or they are rejected or unnoticed, the relationship is in serious trouble because flooding, contempt, and defensiveness are likely to spiral upward.

Warning Sign Six: Bad Memories

If the discouragement and negativity that attend the Four Horsemen and other warning signs have come to dominate the emotional tone of the marriage, even spouses' memories can become distorted under the immense weight of their pessimism. Partners lose access to positive memories and engage in a kind of revisionist history in which they never had much in common, never really had many good times together, never really were close friends, got married for the wrong reasons, stayed married only because raising their children distracted them from their fundamental incompatibility, and probably never really loved one another. One client called this phenomenon "the shit-colored sunglasses" because it contrasted so sharply with the rose-colored lenses through which he and his wife used to view their future together at the beginning of their relationship. This distortion of the past comes as part of the same negative cognitive bias that is common to people in troubled marriages and is behind their criticisms and contempt. Some couples have said that the distortion of their history together destroys their hope because it takes away their last piece of evidence that they were ever truly connected.

As a final note, perhaps one way to characterize Gottman's warning signs is that they are indicators that spouses have begun to lose access to their own complexity and the complexity of their partner. When marital problems are severe, negative moods and patterns become entrenched within the marriage and partners lose access to the positive memories, hopeful expectations, and creative solutions that characterized their relationship in the past. Partners may become one-dimensional to each other and they become blind to one another's positive intentions, good qualities, and the reasons they married in the first place.

PROTECTIVE FACTORS: STRENGTHENING THE BOND

There is hope, however, because the presence of one or more of these warning signs does not assure marital discontent, discord, or dissolution. In fact, Gottman's research tells us clearly that it is not the absence of the warning signs that predicts marital strength, but the presence of seven positive attributes, which function as protective factors against the apocalyptic influence of Four Horsemen and other warning signs. These factors, or what Gottman in his book calls "the seven principles for making marriage work,"[1] are summarized as follows:

1. Spouses know each other's internal lives very well. Each understands the other's motivations, hopes, and dreams. They check in with one another very frequently. They have detailed "love maps" of each other.
2. Spouses "nurture fondness and admiration" for one another. That is, they prioritize keeping their partner's positive attributes in mind, even in the face of conflict.
3. They "turn toward each other instead of away." They view themselves as a team; they make and respond to frequent attempts to connect with one another. For example, they may view doing a chore together as an opportunity to connect rather than simply an unpleasant task.
4. They allow themselves to be influenced by one another. That is, they share power and decision making in the relationship and are open to one another's opinions.
5. They are effective at solving their problems through soft startups, making and receiving repair attempts, soothing one another, compromising, and tolerating each other's differences.
6. They learn to manage and overcome their impasses, or what Gottman calls "unsolvable problems." He believes these are rooted in partners' different dreams and goals that are at odds in the relationship. Couples manage impasses through recognizing and respecting each other's dreams.
7. They "create shared meaning" in their relationship. That is they find a common purpose to their relationship that deepens their connection to one another. This may be around a common spirituality or a common value around parenting, for example.

The importance of these factors is that they create a buffering effect that protects the couple's core emotional bond from the "slings and arrows" that inevitably will assail them. They are described in detail in Gottman's book

The Seven Principles for Making Marriage Work, which I encourage you to read for a more comprehensive understanding of his findings and advice. I believe this is essential reading for couples.

Building off Gottman's work is Brent Atkinson, a marital researcher and faculty member in the Marriage and Family Therapy Program at Northern Illinois University. Atkinson has adapted Gottman's findings and integrated them with the latest research in neurobiology in his approach to couples therapy, called the Pragmatic Experiential Therapy for Couples (PET-C).[2] Atkinson argues that because Gottman's findings are grounded in solid science, therapists can best help couples by helping them to embody Gottman's seven protective principles and avoid the Four Horsemen and other risk factors. As a way to make the protective factors more streamlined and accessible, Atkinson distilled them down to what he calls "the five prerequisites for relationship success" and describes the relationship habits that support them.

Prerequisite 1: A Soft Startup

As we have seen, a harsh startup is an indication that a couple will not resolve a conflict constructively. It follows, then, that couples who start their conflicts respectfully also tend to resolve them satisfactorily. Atkinson suggests that couples are able to do this because partners make a habit of avoiding a judgmental stance toward the other partner, and they are skilled at being able to assert their needs without attacking one another. These couples are able to stick to complaints and avoid the character assassination that comes with criticism. Conflict with these couples isn't necessarily pleasant, but it doesn't escalate into the Four Horseman, and therefore it doesn't cause damage to their emotional connection.

Prerequisite 2: Accepting Influence

The problem with a harsh startup and the Horsemen is that they prevent spouses from listening and responding to one another's legitimate concerns. Partners feel attacked, and so naturally close themselves off to each other's influence. Satisfied couples, on the other hand, are able to listen and respond to one another's requests. These couples often are able to do this because they start with the basic assumption that their partner's concerns and requests are fundamentally legitimate, even if they are different from one's own. Therefore, each makes an honest effort to listen to, understand, and respond to his or her spouse's concerns. In Atkinson's terms, these couples make a habit of "finding the understandable part" of the partner's position and they "give equal regard" to a partner's perspective, even if they don't fully understand or agree with it.

Prerequisite 3: Effective Repair

As noted earlier, Gottman found that couples who don't repair effectively in the midst of conflict are likely to escalate that conflict and ultimately damage the emotional tone of their relationship. Couples who make a habit of offering assurances that they are open to the other's influence are likely to be successful in preventing conflict from spilling over into other areas of their relationship. This doesn't mean that arguments never get ugly with these couples, it just means that they make a point of keeping their arguments in perspective and conveying their openness to one another. An effective repair may be as simple as "I'm really sorry I resorted to name-calling. I really do want to understand your point, I just lost my cool. Can we try again?"

Prerequisite 4: Respecting Your Partner's Dreams, Holding On to Your Own

As noted in Gottman's sixth principle, impasses in relationships are often rooted in partners' different dreams, goals, or expectations about marriage. These may become the basis of repetitive arguments when spouses believe their respective dreams are at odds with one another. For example, newlyweds Rob and Emily came to therapy because they had bitter arguments about how to balance their time as a couple with their social lives. Emily came into the relationship with the expectation that their marriage was a sacred and exclusive place, meant only for the two of them. Her dream for the relationship was that they spend the limited time they had together on the weekends with one another. She wanted to use the time they had together before kids to grow closer and deepen their understanding of one another. She felt there was a narrow window of opportunity to do this before the kids were born and she resented sharing Rob with others. Rob, however, came into the marriage with the expectation that spouses become part of one another's social network. His dream for the relationship was that they go to game nights with friends together, attend each other's family and work functions, and become integrated into the social network of each other's lives. He took pride in "showing off" his new wife to his friends, family, and colleagues. He felt hurt that Emily didn't want to get to know his friends in more than a superficial way. After all, these people had been important to him for many years so it was natural to him that Emily become closer to them. Rob and Emily frequently argued about weekend plans until they recognized that these arguments were symbolic of each other's dreams and expectations. They accepted that there was nothing inherently wrong with the other's dreams. Atkinson suggests that couples who make a habit of understanding and talking about these underlying dreams and expectations are more likely to embody Gottman's sixth principle and negotiate such impasses successfully. These partners start with the assumption that if their spouse is upset, there's a legitimate reason for it that should be explored.

Prerequisite 5: Five Positives for Every Negative

Atkinson's first four prerequisites are focused on successfully managing conflict. His fifth prerequisite is focused on enhancing a couple's connection during nonconflict times. The foundation of this prerequisite lies in Gottman's finding that successful couples have a ratio of at least five positive interactions to every negative interaction. This is sometimes called "The Magic 5:1 Ratio" because if there are four or less positive interactions for every negative, the couple is more likely to encounter difficulties. The implications of this finding are both simple and profound. Couples who wish to take more control of their marital destiny can do so simply by being mindful of this ratio and committing to having five positives for every negative. This is akin to creating buoyancy in a relationship in that couples who maintain this ratio are less likely to get swamped by the oversights, criticisms, mistakes, and missteps that are inevitable in a marriage. In his work with couples, Atkinson encourages them to embody the five-to-one ratio by making habits of being curious about one another's world, being tuned into each other's positives and acknowledging them, pursuing shared meaning, and making and responding to bids for connection.

So what are the implications of these research findings for clergy marriages? Let's start by suggesting that Gottman's findings are equally applicable to clergy and nonclergy relationships because they apply to the processes that foster or erode emotional connection rather than any specific content area. Much more important than the specific topic at issue is the interactional process of a couple that determines how the issue is negotiated. Whether a couple is in conflict about money, sex, the children, work, or a calling is secondary to how they approach resolving it. A couple's nonverbal messages, voice tone and volume, conversational timing and pacing, body posture, facial expressions, and so on convey powerful messages about how they view one another and their relationship. Whether spouses convey respect, openness, and equality is evident in these process details.

Two points may be particularly worthy of consideration for clergy spouses, however. At the very least, one partner has committed a substantial part of his or her life to pursuing a spiritually meaningful endeavor. If partners share similar commitments and expectations about balancing their spiritual and marital lives together, this may provide a wellspring of intimacy renewal and resiliency for their marriage as they pursue shared meaning in a balanced way. If partners have different expectations about balancing the spiritual and marital, however, whether they accept influence from one another becomes critical. Researchers have shown that there's a direct link between marital satisfaction and partners' perceptions of power in the marriage. Specifically, the increase in decision-making equality between husbands and wives in recent decades has resulted in a corresponding increase in marital quality for both partners. Marital quality is likely to decline, however, if a spouse has expectations of equality but doesn't have equal standing in the marital decision-making process.[3] A unique challenge for clergy spouses is that they must negotiate the degree to which their marriage is organized around the clergy partner's calling. As the quotes at the beginning of chapter 3 suggest, the nonclergy partner's career, and consequently aspects of his or her very identity, can become marginalized to the calling if they do not negotiate well. One might argue that this is true in any marriage in which one or both spouses have demanding professions. If God, however, becomes a third party at the table, negotiation becomes an inherently unbalanced process. The spouse with God on his or her side will always be able to claim the moral high road and therefore, "win." But, unlike other arenas in life, the goal of negotiating conflict in a relationship is to have a good relationship, not to win. The research tells us clearly that cost of victory in this situation may be an unsatisfying relationship.

To be sure, these are very complex issues that can only be touched upon here. A starting point, however, in grappling with complex and deeply personal issues is often reflective questioning to add dimension to the issues and the people. Some questions to consider: What are each of your hopes, dreams, and expectations for the marriage? Where did these come from and how did they become important to you? What will be lost if these hopes, dreams, and expectations are not realized? What are the points of divergence and convergence between your dreams? How, in specific behavioral terms, can each of your support the dreams of the other while maintaining your own? If you were to rank order from the least to most difficult the specific ways you could support the others' dreams, what would this list look like? Are there things on the list you're already doing and things you would be willing to start doing within the next week? What is a small request you would make of your partner that would demonstrate his or her support of your dreams if he or she were to agree (think small steps here, not your ultimate wish list)?

Although this has been a rather cursory introduction to Gottman's work and its implications for clergy marriage, hopefully it has provided sufficient grounds for you to begin inventorying your relationship's strengths and concerns.

COMMUNICATION IN MARRIAGE

Perhaps the most common problem bringing couples to therapy is "we just don't communicate." When this is explored in more detail with couples, very often what they describe is that when the partners attempt to express a core need or important concern, they somehow end up mired in arguments that never seem to get resolved and often turn personal.

Standard marital therapy in the past involved teaching a couple communication and problem-solving skills in an attempt to interrupt these argument sequences and overcome the impasses that can happen when partners disagree about how to handle problems. A communication skill commonly taught to couples is sometimes referred to as an "I-statement" or "I-message." This technique requires the partner with a complaint to take responsibility for how he or she feels (as opposed to blaming), express in specific terms why he or she feels that way, and focus on the partner's troubling behavior in a specific circumstance rather than making damaging generalizations (for example, "you never listen") or attributing the concern to generally bad intentions (such as "you knew it would bother me and you did it anyway") or character (for instance, "you only care about yourself") of the partner. This is usually followed by a request for a specific change in behavior.

For example, "Why don't you just take the kids and move back in with your mother if her opinion means so much more to you than mine? Heaven forbid you actually consider there might be other ways to handle things!" becomes "When you made that comment about my parenting to your mother, I felt hurt and undermined because I worry that you don't respect me as a father sometimes." This might be followed with a specific behavioral request or suggestion for both partners, such as "I'd appreciate it if next time you could bring your concerns about how I handle things with the kids to me first and I'll do my best to listen and work with you."

Couples are also frequently taught to use some form of an active listening technique whereby the listener focuses on understanding clearly the speaker's message and confirming his or her understanding with the speaker by reflecting the message back and checking for accuracy. In the preceding example, an active listening statement might sound like "You feel hurt and undermined when I criticize you to my mother. Is this correct? You would like me to bring my concerns to you first to see if we can work it out. Am I close?" Like the I-statement, this technique seems very obvious, but couples in a heated argument frequently do a very poor job of listening to and understanding one another. This is because when people feel attacked, they tend to focus on launching their own counterattack rather than hearing their partner's message. Active listening and I-statements are intended to allow spouses to express their concerns respectfully in order to preempt the negative argument cycles. This in turn will promote the feelings of safety and trust that come with constructive problem solving and healthy compromise.

These techniques look good on paper, right? The problem is couples generally don't communicate about difficult marital and family issues on paper, and even if they did, they would still filter messages through very powerful emotional lenses. Such communication techniques certainly can be useful when the emotional context of the relationship is generally positive and the intensity of arguments is relatively low. They are exceedingly difficult to use, however, when spouses have been conditioned to feel defensive, angry, or simply discouraged by months or years of the Four Horsemen running rough-shod over their marriage. Partners may forget or simply refuse to use techniques and fall back into the usual pattern. Or, because what they're feeling is emotionally incongruent with the techniques, communication at the nonverbal level will disqualify the verbal content of the I-statement or attempts at active listening. An I-statement through clenched teeth or accompanied by rolling one's eyes is not likely to be received as a genuine attempt at constructive communication. In fact, it may be even more harmful to the relationship than the couple's usual arguments. Keep in mind that destructive communication is not simply a failure of will power or a reflection of bad intentions. The work of Gottman, Atkinson, and others tells us clearly that very powerful physiological responses and the very architecture of our brains are working against the use of such techniques in the midst of intense conflict.

This does not mean that there is no place for I-statements, active listening, or any other communication or problem-solving skills. Rather, as Gottman and others suggest, these skills can be used at nonconflict times to enhance connection and trust, or they can be used to prevent the onset of negative communication patterns early in the relationship before such patterns become entrenched. It is also important to keep in mind that good communication skills and problem solving are not sufficient to create a good relationship or undo real damage to a couple's emotional bond. They are primarily helpful to the degree that they support the seven relationship-enhancing factors noted previously and promote an overall sense of positivity and connection between the partners. If, however, despite the couple's best efforts and the best advice from friends and loved ones, the partners are unable to communicate or resolve difficulties satisfactorily, and this is coupled with an air of negativity or distance, it may be helpful to consult with a qualified couples therapist to help evaluate this problem further.

MARITAL THERAPY

By far the most important step spouses can take to preserve and enhance their marriage is to prevent the Four Horsemen and other risk factors from gaining a foothold in the first place. This means committing to incorporating the protective factors discussed earlier in the chapter, being vigilant for the warning signs, and addressing them immediately when they arise. It is important to distinguish here between marital difficulties and true marital problems. It is normal for couples to have unresolved arguments, moments of criticism, feelings of frustration, and hurt feelings. Difficulties become problems, however, when they become systematic and unresolved. That is, when the couple recognizes a difficulty but their attempts to resolve it are unfruitful or even counterproductive, it is likely they may need outside help.

Some important points to consider when seeking a marital therapist are the qualifications of the therapist, the treatment approach he or she uses, and the quality of the relationship between each spouse and the therapist. Unfortunately, there are therapists out there providing marital therapy who have little or no training or experience in treating couples.[4] When looking at credentials, the only way you can be sure that a therapist has sufficient training and experience is to seek a therapist who is a Clinical Member of the American Association for Marriage and Family Therapy (AAMFT). It is also important that the therapist be licensed with the board of mental health in the state in which he or she practices (you may see the designation "LMFT" as part of the credentials of a licensed marriage and family therapist), as this will give you protection as a consumer. There are certainly many skilled couples therapists who are licensed in other professions (for example, clinical social work, psychology, clinical mental health counseling). But you will not be able to ascertain from their credentials alone whether they have training and experience in couples therapy. Thus, if you're seeking couples therapy, be sure to ask any prospective therapist, LMFT or otherwise, about the training and experience that qualifies him or her to help you.

Consumers of marital therapy should also be aware that there are empirically supported treatments available. An empirically supported treatment is one that has research evidence supporting its effectiveness in resolving marital problems. Often this means that there needs to be more than one study showing effectiveness, and at least one study showing effectiveness must be done by someone other than the major founders or proponents of the treatment model.[5] Two of the most well-established treatments are behavioral marital therapy (BMT) and emotionally focused therapy for couples (EFT). BMT typically involves a skill-building component in which couples learn communication and problem-solving skills, and a contracting component, or the negotiation of pleasing behaviors between partners. EFT, on the other hand, focuses on improving relationships and emotional intimacy by shifting partners' problematic emotional reactions and interaction patterns toward ones that produce feelings of closeness. Certainly a therapist can be effective if she or he uses an approach other than BMT or EFT. When a marriage is at stake, however, why not choose a therapist who uses a well-researched, scientifically sound approach to helping you if one is available? At the very least, ask a prospective therapist what approach she or he intends to use in helping you with your marital problems. While the therapist may not use EFT or BMT, he or she should give you an explanation that makes sense to you at an intuitive level.

While the credentials and the specific treatment approach she or he uses are important in determining whether a particular therapist may be helpful, the most important factor for a good therapy outcome is likely to be the quality of the working relationship between the therapist and the couple. Decades of outcome research tells us that the therapeutic alliance is much more important to therapy outcome than any theory or technique.[6] This means not only that both partners should feel a positive emotional connection with the therapist, but that both partners and the therapist agree on the goals of therapy and the tasks of therapy.[7] Questions to consider whether there is a strong therapeutic alliance include: Do both my partner and I feel the therapist is trustworthy, concerned, supportive, interested in both of our perspectives, and invested in helping us? Have we talked directly about the goals for therapy and is this reflected in a treatment plan or an explicit statement about the therapy goals? Does the therapist check in frequently about progress toward goals? Are the therapist's rationales for in-session interventions and out-of-session homework tasks clear? Are the interventions and tasks linked clearly to our goals in coming to therapy?

Couples therapists often hear stories from clients about their previous therapists who seemed well intentioned or seemed to have good ideas but ultimately failed to help them reach their treatment goals. Sometimes, despite the best training, credentials, and treatment approach, there is simply a lack of fit between the therapist and one or both of the clients. It is imperative that *both* partners agree that the therapist is helpful if the therapy is going to be effective. Sometimes it takes a bit of shopping around before you end up with someone who is a good fit for both of you. Research tells us that most change in therapy tends to happen within in the first one to seven sessions, and if clients don't experience change early on in therapy, they are much less likely to benefit from that therapy over the long term.[8] Consequently, you should not hesitate to end a therapy if you don't have a confident feeling within the first few sessions that the therapist can help you. A good therapist should be able to get to the issues most relevant to you both in the first session, convey a sense that he or she understands your concerns and goals, and offer a general direction for therapy by the end of the second session. Some general questions to consider include: Do you have a clear feeling (within the first one or two sessions) that this person can help us? Are the sessions fair and balanced in that the therapist does not appear to be consistently taking one person's side over the other or giving one person more leeway to monopolize the time? Is the therapist able to engage both you and your partner in the process? Do you feel understood and safe? Because of the intensity of couples' conflicts, it is vitally important that the therapist be able to block the destructive patterns that brought you to therapy from taking over the therapeutic process. If you feel the therapy is "more of the same" problem, just in a therapist's office, raise this concern with the therapist immediately. If it continues despite everyone's best efforts, it may be time to consider a different therapist.

As a last point, it is crucial that you not put off getting help if you notice some of the warning signs indicated in this chapter and you have not had success in addressing them on your own. Couples frequently tell their therapist that they have been dealing with relationship problems for years before they decided to make an appointment. Often couples have become so emotionally reactive to one another that they cannot communicate civilly about the really charged issues, even when they both are trying genuinely to do so. Even worse, one or both partners have withdrawn from the relationship to such a degree they don't even have the energy to argue. The chances of therapy resuscitating a marriage that has lost its pulse are indeed slim. It is crucial that couples seek help before negativity poisons their relationship to the point where they are emotionally deadened to one another. The more negative the relationship has become, the more likely it is to resist efforts to reshape it in positive ways. Seek help before this happens. In spite of how difficult things can get, it is encourging when couples still have enough passion to fight with one another. No matter how dirty it gets, it's still a sign that the relationship has life and energy that can be redirected toward reclaiming the feelings and strengths that brought these two people together in the first place.

CONCLUSION

This chapter has offered a brief introduction to what every couple should know. Please read for yourself the original work of John Gottman and other authors in the recommended resources, as that material is much more nuanced and comprehensive than what can be provided within the confines of one chapter. These particular resources were chosen because they are based in established theory, research, and practice from the marital literature but are also accessible, relevant, and user-friendly. Within them you will find general knowledge on relationships as well as some very specific, concrete advice on strengthening your emotional connection and avoiding the most common marital pitfalls. Hopefully the information offered here has provided some grounds for new reflection and dialogue about the unique and complex realities of clergy partnerships.

Seven

What about the Kids?

Dear God,

This night, I give my children back to you in the hope and faith that you will return them to me in the morning to love and to raise. They were yours before mine, they are yours now, and their futures are held in your hands. Hold us all in your love. In Christ's name, Amen.

> My seventh grader and several of his friends decided to cut down a dying bush one day. Unfortunately, it wasn't in my yard or the yards of any of the other children, but in the front yard of a neighbor's home. All the kids involved got into trouble, and all of them had to repair the damage as best as they could—in addition to other consequences. The story was big news in the church, but with a twist. The only child mentioned was my son, the minister's kid who behaved so badly. The others were forgotten, but for years comments were made about my boy.

> The church had a special dinner for visiting missionaries, followed by Greek line dancing. The teens of the church had served the dinner and were in the back of the room. None of them showed any interest in joining the adults who were dancing. At the end of the first dance, the pastor's wife stood in the middle of the room and angrily

gestured to her two teen daughters to leave the others and join in the dancing. It was embarrassing for the girls to be forced into doing something that no other teens were expected to do.

> Sometimes I feel that the congregation expects my kids to be perfect because my wife is the minister. Comments are made when they miss church events or make noise during the service. The scrutiny is a bit much.[1]

Fostering a life is an extraordinary experience, bringing untold blessings and unexpected joy. It is a way to give something unique to the world, to make it a better place by loving more and raising a child to be compassionate. Having children binds a couple together in a new way; there is a living, breathing, thinking, loving connection that was not there before. The nature of the world changes with the coming of a child. It will change with the advent of each new child. One could say that the entire universe changes with each baby, human and otherwise, because new possibilities arise that were not there before. This is true when an infant arrives, and true when an older child becomes part of the family. Whether a couple receives a child through birth, adoption, or foster care, the blessing of parenthood is the blessing of fostering a life with heartfelt prayer.

When children come into a marriage, things get complicated. This is true for all families, clergy and otherwise. Before children, a couple has more free time to spend together, to pursue careers, to keep in touch with extended family, and to be active participants in the community. With the advent of a first child, and with each additional child after that, the couple loses the time, the energy, and the freedom to go about their pre-procreation lives. Careers may be pursued, community duties performed, family matters attended to, and nights out without children scheduled. But all of these things now require advanced planning, child care, and additional funds to pay for it all. Unless Mary Poppins happens to belong to the family, gone are the days of spontaneous movie dates and a drink at the local pub. The great joy of children comes with a great responsibility that weighs heavily on the social calendar, work schedule, and bank account. Multitasking becomes a necessity every day, with laundry done while a child naps, work scheduled during school hours every week, and dinner prepared while quizzing a teen for tomorrow's algebra test. The energy and devotion required to raise a child or multiple children is something most couples cannot imagine when they have only each other to consider. The adventure that is parenthood should be undertaken with great humility and optimism—as should any relationship that connects the bodies, minds, hearts, and spirits of others.

For those raising a child in the context of Christian faith, things become much more difficult and much easier.[2] It is more difficult because the care of the spirit becomes the foundation of life. Tending to the child's spirit takes time and a concerted effort. Bringing a child into the community of faith in more than a cursory way requires showing up for worship, Sunday school, and other ongoing communal activities. As a child reaches school age, these things begin to conflict with school events, sports schedules, and homework. The world does not take into account the worship life of the faith community, and difficult choices must be made. Should a child be on a soccer team if the games are every Sunday morning? Can a teen go to youth group on a school night if homework remains undone? Is there plenty of time for playing—something necessary for the heart, mind, body, and soul of everyone?[3] Making decisions about all of these things, when the right answer is not always obvious, can be a burden that weighs heavily on parents. There is no single right way to raise a child, and no way to know if the right decisions are always made. Children complicate the lives of their parents because life choices are not simple nor always easily lived out. That is why many parents stay up nights wondering how their decisions will mess their children up for life.

Faith also makes nurturing the life of a child easier. Parents whose faith forms the basis for their lives know that their children first belong to God. Decisions that foster the spirits of their children, choices that respect the integrity of mind and body, come before other goals. If God is the creator of all that is, then children are God's first, and the enormous burden of being everything for the children is removed. Children's lives are held by God, as are the parents' lives. This larger context provides parents and children with something beyond themselves and their own interests; they are not alone in the universe, nor are they responsible for controlling everything that occurs in their lives. Prayerfully, parents make decisions for their children to the best of their ability. The rest is turned over to God. Faith makes it easier to accept things beyond the control of parental oversight and can help parents to see their role as a gift from God and a responsibility to God and the world. The task of parenting is not to create a perfect world for children, but to help children see Christ's presence in themselves and in others.

GREAT PARENTAL EXPECTATIONS

What do we want for our children? It is a question that parents ask, often before a child enters their lives. When a couple begins talking about raising a child, expectations are voiced. Most want a healthy child, able to grow without disease or disability. There are behavioral expectations, too. Parents hope that their children will learn to be considerate, treating others with kindness. Hopes that a child will have confidence and the ability to accomplish goals are common. Many parents pray for a child who is loving, capable, and a credit to the family, the community, and the world. That their child will not fall victim to bullies at school and will not take advantage of others are reasonable expectations.

There are many wonderful and informative books on childhood development, education, and psychology.[4] There are books on the spirituality of childhood.[5] These are resources for parents, providing a larger context for their expectations as they nurture a child. They can help parents and caregivers understand the stages of childhood development so that a child is not expected to accomplish things beyond his or her ability. A quick trip to a local library or a cruise on the Internet can provide parents with more than enough information, so the particulars of general parenting skills and childhood development are not necessary in this book. What will be addressed is how parenting can be placed within the context of faith and how parenting is affected by ordained ministry. There is no one correct way to create a loving family life, but asking and living into the answers of these questions may be helpful.

AM I LIVING IN THE PRESENT TENSE WITH MY CHILD?

> Then little children were being brought to him in order that he might lay his hands on them and pray. The disciples spoke sternly to those who brought them; but Jesus said, "Let the little children

> come to me, and do not stop them; for it is to such as these that the kingdom of heaven belongs." And he laid his hands on them and went on his way. (Matt. 19:13–15)

There is no minimum age requirement for coming to Jesus. Usually, this passage serves as a reminder to the faith community that children are important; it is not common for it to be considered part of the parent/child relationship. Because the family is the first faith community for a child, this passage can be quite helpful, when seen in a different way.

Children are noisy. They require a great amount of work, and they do not necessarily contribute to the family finances or ease the workload of their parents. They are not adults and cannot contribute to the family life what an adult can in terms of skill or knowledge. Every few months, children change shoe sizes, heights, and ways of reasoning. Childhood is an ever-changing, impermanent state. What a child needs changes from year to year, keeping parents in a constant state of readjustment. Because of this, it is tempting to settle for getting through the present while keeping the focus on a future time when adulthood arrives. The emphasis shifts from the present, changing context to a future, more stable time. With this shift, children become potential adults, big people in the making; childhood is really pre-adulthood, a span of years that must be crossed before getting to the adulthood on the other side.

If this line of thought continues, a child becomes potential incarnate, growing toward the fulfillment of adulthood. With this reasoning, parents must keep their focus on the future, tailoring the present in such a way as to achieve a good outcome: a successful, functioning adult. This is why it is critical to establish college funds, encourage or insist on participation in school government and sports, and to make sure solid scores are achieved in the critical standardized tests. There is little time from birth to high school graduation, and none of that time can be wasted. Exposure to foreign lands and languages is a must if a child is to be well-rounded. Every advantage and every opportunity must be taken. To do anything less as a parent is to fail, and failure is unacceptable. This attitude of "everything before maturity is a necessary but difficult prelude to life" is a sad, flawed way of understanding children's lives.

It is important to take the future into account when raising a child, but when the quest for future success discounts present life, it is damaging. If a child's life is all about accomplishing goals, then he or she comes to believe that human value is something to be earned rather than something innate. No child should feel that self-worth is something that must be earned over and over again, that every day he or she must prove worthy of taking up space on the earth and consuming oxygen. The fact that the child is in the world, a unique presence, is the ground for fundamental worth. If orientation to future success robs a child of this most basic truth, something much more precious than worldly success is lost. A child's present existence should lead into the future, not be sacrificed to it.

It is this truth, the value of the child's present, that the disciples forgot. For them, the blessing of a child was not as important as other acts. Their attempts to keep the children and those who brought them away from Jesus show a disregard for the spiritual needs of children. Not only does Jesus welcome the children, but he goes one better: he declares that the kingdom of heaven belongs to them! They cannot provide Jesus with food or shelter, they have no influence over authority, but Jesus does not tell them to come back when they are grown. Jesus blesses them, lays hands on them, and reminds his own disciples that the kingdom of heaven is theirs. Children belong with Jesus, children have the kingdom of heaven as their right. Without the same external worth as most adults, children are worthy of heaven to Jesus—as they are, not as potential adults. In the present, not only in the future. They are enough, they are sufficient, they are a delight to Jesus for who they are, not for what they can do.

For parents, this should be a great relief and a reason for celebration. Their children are already loved and accepted by God, just as they themselves are.[6] As parents, teaching children the sacred truth that Jesus loves them is much more important than any other task. This does not remove the work necessary to raise a child; what it does is place parenting in the larger truth of God's love and Jesus' blessing for every child. The anxiety that drives parents to seek perfection for their child (and often from their child) can be given up because it is of no eternal value. Jesus welcomes every child in the present, not in the future. Parenting should reflect this by valuing the ever-changing present for itself, not for the success it might earn in the future.[7] Never forget that Jesus blesses now, not only in adulthood. Accepting the child's present and living into the blessings it holds is the lesson to learn from Jesus.

What does this look like in practical terms? The details depend upon the time, location, and life situation of the family. It comes down to a perspective rather than a particular action, but some examples may be helpful. Living in the present means that a father reads to his diaper-clad daughter not because it will one day make it easier for her to read and develop abstract reasoning skills (although this will be a result): a father reads to his daughter because it is a joy to share a story that the girl loves in this time and in this place. He will read the same story about cows until the cows come home because she likes the pictures and the sound of his voice. The future benefits are not lost on the father, but they do not hold him and his daughter captive. The future does not rob the present of its blessing, even in so common an activity.

A mother spends time with her son building skyscrapers with wooden blocks, rolling cans across the kitchen floor, and chasing fireflies around the yard. This play will help him develop hand-eye coordination, sharpen fine motor skills, and strengthen gross motor skills. But these benefits are side issues, not the central focus. The time spent in play is for the play itself and for the delight that mother and son experience in the game and in each other.

Living in the present and allowing a child to flourish in the present is not short-sighted, nor does it imply a careless attitude toward the future. A mother and father who live in the present with their child, valuing the here and now rather than being distracted by future possibilities, reveal their trust in God's constant care. God delights in a child, and in parents, not for accomplishments future or past; God delights in who each person is, not primarily or merely in what they can do.

GIVING LIFE, TAKING LIFE

When a couple brings a child home, by whatever method, life is permanently changed. So much time and effort go into caring for the child, and the love that comes into the family is something that did not exist before. This is true of each additional child as well. Parents sacrifice time, energy, financial resources, and great effort to provide a good home for each child. Both parents are fundamentally changed because they became parents. This is true of all deep relationships, but perhaps especially true with a parent and child because of the daily responsibility involved. The needs of a child are such a central part of life and its activities that the interests and pursuits of parents as individuals often become secondary, reclaimed later when the children mature. When children grow up and leave the home, or when they remain in the home as autonomous adults, they no longer require as much energy and attention. What happens then?

No couple can return to their preprocreation days because of the aging process, the parenting adventure, and the work that has been done over the child's lifetime. Circumstances require a new way of being a couple, and new ways of being individuals. This can be the next great adventure for a couple, but courage is required. The life of primary caretaker and primary provider for children must be given up for the couple to set out on a new path and for the children to be given over to their adult lives. This does not mean that the parents don't tend to their adult children's needs when necessary and appropriate, but that their children's major life decisions and directions cannot be made by the parents. This is a wrenching experience for many parents, and a time of great stress for their children. Not all choose to embrace their post–primary caretaker identity, and some do not recognize their child's adulthood with any sense of grace. Clinging to a stage that has passed robs some of future dreams and joys.

Much of the anguish that comes with letting children become independent adults stems from the mistaken notion that the child's life is a gift that the parents give to themselves. The child comes through the parents, but his or her life is not their possession. A child is a separate but intimately related individual, not a means to correct the mother's past mistakes or achieve a father's unfulfilled dreams. In other words, the child does not exist for the sake of the parents; the child exists for his or her own sake, to be a delight to God and a gift to the family.

A second mistaken notion is that the parent's whole reason for existing in this world is to be the parent to a child. When a child becomes the sole focus and purpose of a parent's life, the parent cannot see any life beyond the child. The child means everything to the parent, taking center stage in all thought and action. This puts enormous pressure upon a child because he or she must bear the burden of the parent's life as well as live his or her own. If a child fails in one pursuit or another, it is not merely a failure to accomplish a goal, but a failure to provide the parent with a successful reason to live.

Both of these notions are idolatrous because both deny the child's individuality and separate reality. Either the child is an instrument in parental achievement or the parent is just the means of bringing the child into the world. In either case, the central truth that both parent and child are God's first has been lost. People are given to one another for love and support, not to provide a second chance at life or a reason to live. God gives life, God holds that life, and God will take life into eternity. No parent can do this, nor should he or she make the attempt. When parents allow God to be God, and their child to be God's first, then they are free to be good parents. They are free to continue living meaningful lives after the kids become adults.

BEING AND DOING

While parents hope that their child will grow to do many interesting, exciting, and worthwhile things in life, what a child does as a child and as an adult is not the sum of his or her worth. Meaningful work and other accomplishments are wonderful, but they are not equal to the worth of any person —child or adult. Who a child is will always be more than a sum of achievements or abilities. To lose sight of this is to confuse the value of *being* with the arithmetic of *doing*. No child is worthwhile merely because he or she can perform certain tasks or acquire valuable skills in the future. A child is valued because he or she is a gift of God, not primarily for what he or she can do for the world.[8] Human value is *innate*, something that everyone is born with rather than earns.

A child should never feel that the love of his or her parents must be earned. Parental love should be freely given, just as God's love is freely given. Love, respect, and worth are not bargaining chips to be used in the quest to achieve worldly success: they are the foundation of a solid relationship between parent and child. This is based in God's love for every person and should reflect this love. What a child accomplishes in life can never be the foundation for a blessed, fulfilling life: it can only be the response to it, something that grows out of it. Jesus welcomes children to him and blesses them, not for something that they can accomplish, but for their value as beloved creatures of God. Parents who remember that love and respect are given, not earned, keep a better perspective about their children's worldly successes and failures. They also have an easier time remembering that they, too, are loved for who they are, not what they do.

With the foundational truth that a child's worth is based upon his or her existence rather than accomplishments, parents can be more realistic in the expectations they have for their child. Whether a child reads early, plays soccer well, or can sing on key does not determine his or her value to God, parents, or the world. They are a wonderful extra. The pressure to hurry a child along, to push for more practice, to expect abilities beyond reach, goes away. Rather than molding a child to conform to a particular vision of success, parents are free to allow the child's natural talents and interests to grow. This does not mean that parents should not help a child achieve developmentally appropriate skills, but it does mean that the parent thinks no less of a slow reading child than one who can read at age four. Life skills are important, but not the value of a child. Parents should support their children, encourage them in their pursuits, and hold them to their responsibilities out of love and a realistic set of expectations. It is vital that a parent not withdraw love and support when a child does not meet expectations. To reduce a child to what he or she is capable of implies that less capable children are less valuable. This is patently false and can lead to denying the full humanity of those who will never achieve worldly success. Parents should follow Jesus' lead in this, gathering their children to them and blessing them without reservation.

PREACHER'S KIDS AND COMMUNITY EXPECTATIONS

Ministers' children are often called PKs—short for preacher's kids or pastor's kids. Without any say in the matter, these children live in relation to the worship community. Whether they belong to the congregation that hired their clergy mother or father, or whether they attend another with their non-clergy parent, their lives are affected by the vocational choices made by their parents. Their presence or absence from the community life is noted, sometimes drawing critical or complimentary comments. Adults in the worship community may recognize them and talk with them more than the other young people in church. There may be expectations that the PKs will join many if not all the groups for children their age. Their behavior is noted more often than the behavior of the other children, sometimes commented upon and sometimes not. In general, they are observed more closely than other children because their father or mother is an ordained minister of the church. People seem more surprised if a PK falls short of expectations than if another child does.

The fact of expectations within the community is not a problem. Any couple who raises a child in the church community will be encouraged to have their child participate in Sunday school programs, pageants, choirs, and youth groups. Parents choose to participate in the communal life of the church and choose to have their children participate, too. When a child is baptized, parents promise to bring their child to church and to raise him or her in the Christian faith. It is only when the line between the ordained ministry of the parent and the faith life of the PK becomes blurred that a problem arises. Is the child seen as an extension of the ministering parent, a part of the "minister's family" that is supposed to provide an ideal picture of faith, hope, and happiness? Is the child expected to participate in the ministry of the church as a default assistant to the father or mother? When the child's presence and participation is seen as a given rather than as the choice of the child, expectations have gone awry.

While it is quite acceptable to hold a PK to his or her duties when he or she chose to participate in a ministry, it is unfair to expect him or her to "fill in" for another child in a task the PK did not sign up for in the first place. For example, asking a PK to switch weeks as a youth usher is fine if he or she willingly signed up to participate in that ministry; asking a PK to be a youth usher when he or she has not signed up to participate in that program in the first place is not. Most adults would be unhappy if they were asked to fill in as an usher if they were not willing volunteers. These adults would not be criticized if they did not "fill in" for another adult on short notice. The same goes for their children. Why should it be any different for a PK? When a worship community or the ordained minister takes the participation of a PK for granted, treating their work as the back-up for everyone else, he or she is being taken advantage of.[9]

When the church community or a child's parents expect him or her to devote time, talent, and energy to church activities without recognizing that as the child's contribution and the child's choice, then that PK becomes merely an extension of the parent's ministry. This is similar to how some clergy spouses and partners are treated, but even less acceptable because a child has little choice in such matters. While a partner or spouse may object or refuse to be the unpaid assistant, a child is not free to do so. The need to please a parent and to gain approval far outweighs the freedom of choice for most children. When being a "good" child is dependent upon working at the church, a PK is being treated unfairly.

The behavior of a pastor's child may be noticed more than the behavior of other children. This is understandable in one sense because most of the community members will know the child while they may not know the other children in the church. This is especially true if there are multiple services, some of which few children attend. The adults in the relatively child-free services will not have an opportunity to learn the names of most children in the church because they never encounter them. The minister's child will be recognized because he or she belongs with the leader of the church.

When the recognition of the pastor's kids moves from recognition to judgment of behavior, things can go wrong. In some instances, PKs are expected to be model children. Their actions are scrutinized in ways that the other children's actions are not. Harsher judgment may be passed on PKs because they are expected to uphold an ideal image of what a minister's family should do and be. Requiring perfection in all actions in all times and places is unrealistic; it becomes unrealistic and grossly unfair if the minister's child is the only one held to such an impossible standard. Leading the community is the ministry of the parent, not the burden of the child. If community expectations become too difficult or too vocal, the spirit of the child is adversely affected. What does it profit the church community to gain a well-behaved PK if the child loses his or her soul?

A second possibility is that the PK is judged more leniently than other children within the faith community. In these instances, a child is not held to the same standards as the other children in the community. Rude behavior is tolerated because no one wants to upset the clergy parent. Sunday school teachers, youth leaders, and choir directors do not feel comfortable addressing unacceptable behavior. They allow the PK to miss practices and events that others are expected to attend. This, too, is unhealthy because parameters are being changed just because the parent is a minister. It is not about the child's well-being, but about the parent's position. This can build up resentment among the other children, making group activities less appealing and effective. While the PK may be "getting away" with bad behavior (or being praised more than the others for the same activities and actions), he or she will not be developing the skills and openness necessary for fruitful friendships. The child is separated from the other children by his or her own actions and the reactions of the adults involved.

For the child, the parents, and the community, there is a danger in treating a PK differently than other children. For the child, a distinction develops that separates him or her from other children. He or she never gets to be just one of the group. Always there is the shadow of parental ordained ministry that colors participation in community events. If the parents and community leaders are not careful to treat a PK as they treat other children, the PK may never have the joy of being a member of the group—just like everyone else. That is a precious thing to lose, and may lead the child to resent the community and the Christian faith.

Parents want their child to succeed. They hope their child will join group activities in positive ways, and that he or she will be treated kindly by other children and adults. For a minister and spouse, the danger lurks in their expectations. If parents are raising a child to meet an internalized ideal vision of what a minister's child is supposed to be, they make a serious mistake. When parents feel that their child's every action or remark enhances or detracts from an ideal, they are in danger of valuing the image over the reality of their child. Every child will do and say wonderful things. Every child will do and say things that shock. Every child needs to know what is acceptable and what is not. What every child does not need is to be held to a standard that is beyond reason, a standard that does not foster spiritual, emotional, and physical well-being. A child, whether a PK or not, is not a preshrunk adult. When parents react to a child not for his or her own sake but for the sake of an idealized vision of what that child should be, they do damage. Parents must raise the child they have, not the child that the community expects a minister to have.

For the faith community, the minister's child can cause conflict. When the child is seen as the default assistant for his or her parent, the community does a grave disservice. When a PK is valued or evaluated in ways other children within the community are not, then the child is not seen as an individual, but as an element of the pastor's ministry. The child becomes a model or a warning, something to be judged rather than just one among many youth in the community. The fundamental equality of all within the community is challenged and found wanting. This does not reflect the foundational truth that God values all people and that Jesus loves everyone equally.

Many times, people within the faith community do not consciously treat PKs differently from the other children. Their actions are unconscious, making them much harder to address. Whether the PKs are judged by higher behavioral standards or allowed to "get away" with things others are not, the inequality must be addressed. A good way to bring this inequality to light is to ask a very simple question: Would I react the same way if this were someone else's child? A second question can help clarify things even more: Are my actions for the benefit of the child, or for the benefit of the clergy parent? When these questions are asked and answered honestly, a PK has a much better chance of being seen as separate from his or her minister parent. No community should place the burden of parental ordained ministry on the backs of children, and no parent should treat his or her child as a means to further ministerial goals.

OUTSIDE ISSUES TO CONSIDER

In previous chapters, the transient nature of ministry has been addressed. Clergy spouses and partners relocate for various calls, in some denominations more than others. While this is difficult for the partner, it can be even more challenging for a child. There may not be any family close enough to visit on a regular basis. The only constant factor is the nuclear family, which puts great pressure on all involved to provide support and stability with few outside anchors. This does not mean that PKs will grow up to be insecure or look back upon their early years as full of tribulation, but it does mean that creating a fruitful and nurturing environment can be difficult. These are three related issues concerning children and relocation that must be addressed: change of schools, change of surrounding community, and change of faith community.

Changing schools

When a clergy family relocates, the children must leave their old schools to continue their education in a new place. Friends and routine extracurricular activities are left behind, and children enter a new and foreign educational environment. School standards and curricula vary from place to place, significantly changing the school experience. The child may find that he or she has already exceeded the standards of the new school, or that he or she is expected to work at a higher level. Even the subject matter may change. For example, Latin America may be the focus of sixth grade social studies in one system, while Europe might be the focus in another. Even if the same subjects are addressed in both systems, they may be addressed in a different order, from different perspectives, and in different grade levels. This can cause difficulties for a child entering a new school.

In addition to the larger issues of school standards and curricula, there are everyday things that become sources of anxiety. Where does the bus stop? Is there a dress code? If there is no uniform, what do the kids here wear? Things like navigating the cafeteria lines and finding a place to sit for lunch can be overwhelming. The truth is that the routine of school can vary enough to make the transition from one school to another challenging.

There are advantages to being the new kid in school. There is an air of mystery about a new student that can give him or her an opening into new friendships. School becomes an adventure that involves discovering new people and new possibilities for growth. The PK learns firsthand that daily customs and routines are not the same everywhere, and that the world is infinitely more complex and interesting than most people realize. A child also discovers that he or she can adapt and live a good life in more than one location. The possibilities of what home looks like are many, and a child who relocates may grow into a more adventurous adult.

There are disadvantages to relocation that accompany the new school adventure. Depending upon the age of the child, developmental issues come into play. It is very difficult to lose a circle of friends in the teen years. Academic expectations or school policy concerning new students may place a child in a lower level class than he or she is accustomed to—or in a higher level that goes beyond what a child can do. The sense of self as capable comes into question, and may make the child anxious about the future.

Friendships may not form quickly and may never provide the support left behind in the other community.

While many of these issues may seem insignificant to the parents, they can be staggeringly important to a child. Recognizing the child's fears and hopes is crucial, even in the midst of unpacking boxes and establishing a new working environment.

Changing the Surrounding Community

Sometimes the community surrounding the new church is similar in composition to the one left behind. It may be in the same geographical region, it may have similar socioeconomic factors, and it may be similar in the population density. At the same time, it may not be the same in any of these areas. When these factors change, children must adapt to a new reality. This means that the usual activities and community resources may not be available, and that new possibilities can be explored. It takes time and effort to become familiar with the new community, and that time can be stressful.

The loss of familiar territory can cause great pain for a child. Simple things that do not upset an adult may make a child anxious. For example, one PK recounted the difficulty he had in adjusting to a rural community in northern New York after living in central New Jersey. His new home was on a back road and had none of the ambient noise or light that his former house had. While he was used to sleeping with the street lights shining in his window and the commuter train rumbling by regularly, he was frightened by the darkness of the night in the new community. The lack of mechanical noise and the presence of wildlife sounds upset him for months. He eventually adjusted and came to love the new area, but the transition time was a trial for him.

The social and economic factors in the new community may have a profound effect upon a minister's child, especially if they are very different from those in the place left behind. The standards of living may be different, and the type and amount of material possessions considered average may change. For a minister's child, this may mean that he or she is no longer on an equal footing with the children in the community. If a child suddenly finds the family standard of living much lower or higher than the community, it may be difficult to fit in. This is especially true when a minister moves a family to an area that is affluent beyond what a minister's and partner's combined income can meet. A child may not be able to participate in the activities of his or her peers, making it more difficult to find a group of friends. While there are very good reasons why a minister might take an underpaid call in a wealthy community, that decision affects the children as much as it does the parents. Parents must recognize that the child is paying a cost for the underpaid call. It is vital that the child does not feel that he or she is worth less as an individual just because others have more money.

With a change in community comes a change in customs. Accents can change with the move, making the newness of the PK noticeable every time he or she speaks. Every day behavior may not be the same. Is it common to greet strangers when passing them on the street? How much eye contact is too much? Are adults addressed as "ma'am" and "sir" by children? These regional differences can be a source of great amusement and fun, but also produce anxiety. The possibility of rejection accompanies the child in these new surroundings in a way that it did not in the old, familiar community. Parents should take note of this, and take seriously the anxiety of their child as everyone gets used to the new community.

Changing the Faith Community

When a new call is taken, a new faith community becomes the context for the minister and his or her children. This is true whether the children attend that church or seek another. With a new church come new worship practices and new people leading the children's activities. Sunday school classes are different, and the church service may feel unfamiliar. The youth group may focus on very different activities and meet on a different night. The customs of each faith community are unique to it, even while having a lot in common with other churches. These differences may not be significant in the overall scheme of life, but for a child already facing a change in school, local community, and home, these differences may seem much more important. It is vital that the child feel welcome in the faith community. Although the worship life may be different, it is a way to seek and serve God.[10] The faith life of the child is important and should not be forgotten in the rush to fulfill a parent's call to serve Christ and the world through an ordained ministry.

TO WHOM WILL THEY TURN?

Everyone needs pastoral care, including minister's children. But who is their pastor if the minister of their church is their parent? They need an outside pastor to serve as a guide, to discuss spiritual issues and to provide a pastoral presence in times of trouble. These things cannot be provided by a parent, especially if the child's pastoral issue concerns the parents! This is especially true as a child grows into adulthood.[11] It is an irony of the minister's family life that a call to serve the spiritual needs of others often results in the discounting and neglect of the PK's spiritual life and needs. No child should have to go without pastoral care and a sense of Christian community just because a father or mother is living out a baptismal ministry through ordained ministry.

The spiritual life of a pastor's child may not present much of a problem until the teen years arrive. At that point, questions arise and doubts need to be discussed. When a child's parent is a pastor, the child may not feel able to express doubt or rebel from the faith handed to him or her. This rebellion, this questioning of faith, is natural and necessary. It is only through questioning, through intentional thinking about faith, that a child can claim the faith for himself or herself. This time of questioning, this opportunity for rebellion and acceptance, may be unavailable to a PK if the cost is too high. If parental affection and community approval are at stake, a child may not have the strength or the opportunity to reject or claim the Christian faith. What a terrible price to pay! This is a price that others are not asked to pay, so why ask it of a PK?[12]

For some parents, this time of questioning is too risky: what if the child chooses to live a faith life that does not reflect the parents' choices? What if their child seeks another church tradition or another religion, or chooses to reject organized religion altogether? It comes down to a matter of trust: do parents trust God and their children enough to let them work out their relationship apart from parental control? The truth is that parents do not stand between their children and God, controlling their interactions to produce an acceptable and manageable outcome. Parents pray for their children, love and raise their children, in God's all-encompassing embrace. They are held together in God's love, and to suppose differently is to deny God's grace and the children's right to a one-on-one relationship with God through Christ. Letting children grow into their own relationships with God requires the parents to trust God and to give up trying to be God for their offspring.

What happens when a child rejects the parents' faith tradition, choosing a different Christian tradition, a different faith, or rejecting religion as a whole? This will cause pain because most parents want their children to experience the same life-giving faith that they find so vital. But it is arrogant and presumptuous to believe that a parent can judge how and when a child will come to faith. It takes great trust to allow a child to be God's first, whatever that may look like. But what other choice is there for parents raising a child in faith? Ordained ministry does not excuse a parent from letting his or her child live the life that God wants for that child. The most loving thing to do is to give up the illusion of control over the movement of the Spirit in a child's life, and to admit that God and the child will work out their relationship on their own schedule and in their own way. If a child chooses another church, explores other ways of praying to God, or questions the existence of God, it is not a choice made to irritate or cause pain to the parents. The choice is about the child's spiritual life and God's infinite love. Unless the child has chosen a dangerous cult or some form of faith that causes physical, emotional, psychological, or spiritual damage, parents should honor the choice. This may be the child's way of finding a pastor and a community of faith that is solely his or her own, not an extension of the ordained ministry of one parent and the faith choices of the other. A move of religious independence is not necessarily meant to reject the parents' faith; it may just be the move to accepting faith as an independent adult. This choice may mean the loss of the family faith routine, but it may be absolutely the most faithful choice a child can make. Whether a child chooses to remain in the parents' faith community or join another, God holds that child fast as he or she moves from a child's faith to an adult's faith. When parents accept the faith decisions of their child, they allow their child to grow up, moving into compassionate adulthood and the lifelong adventure of maturing faith.

LETTING GO OF THE CHILDREN

God willing, children grow up. Most grow out of their toddler years, learn to read and write, go through puberty, and become adults. The things that they require from their parents change as they grow, and eventually they choose their own life paths. It is difficult for many parents to recognize and honor the reality of their adult children's lives because then the parents must confront the truth that they cannot protect them from the world. Their children will suffer loss; they will lose friends and have to find their own ways to be faithful to God. They will make choices and perhaps have their own children. Parents cannot control their children's lives, nor should they try. There is enormous grace in giving a child over to God and encouraging a child to go out into the world to live in faith. Prayerfully always, tearfully often, parents must hand over the responsibility for life choices to the adult child. Parents should honor the child's right to make his or her own life decisions, even if that means making mistakes. It takes great trust in God to let a child live out his or her own unique call to baptismal ministry. Trust God with the life of the adult child. God's love for that child is steadfast, even when it works itself out in unexpected ways. Jesus gathered the children to him, and will continue to embrace them as they grow into adulthood.

But what about children who will never live independently? How do parents let go of these children, trusting God to hold them when they cannot care for themselves? No faith, no ministry, can guarantee a healthy, capable child. But even with these children, God's love and relationship is direct, not redirected through the parent. It is infinitely harder to trust the lives of these children to God and the world because they do need compassionate care beyond the needs of most people. The dreams of the parents for these children must be of a different nature, although no less valuable. All children, regardless of ability, have a spirit that belongs to God. All children, regardless of ability, are created in God's image. Letting go of the fear for the future of these children, living in the hope and trust that they will be taken care of when the parents are gone are the faith challenges that the parents must face. Parents must do what they can to foster the faith and life of their children but, in the end, trust that God holds them fast.

When the people brought their children to Jesus for a blessing, they released them to Christ's embrace. Parents cannot release their children to God's love without letting them go. The Spirit leads children to Jesus for blessing when parents let them go. As with all things, God transforms what is released in faith and hope, returning it in unexpectedly blessed ways. PKs, like all children, belong to God. This is the truth of faith: God loves and God holds everyone from birth to death. Is there a greater gift to give a child than this truth?

Eight

Foundation of Life

This is the easiest and most difficult chapter to write and perhaps to read. In the other chapters, specific issues have been highlighted, common experiences reviewed, and suggestions given for a deeper understanding of how the ordination of one partner affects the life of the other. These last pages are about faith, and the joys and risks of living a life in covenant relationship with another. It is about deep matters of the heart and spirit, and how those matters can be blessed or broken by the difficulties of being a clergy spouse or partner.

Whether these pages are read from a place of trust and confidence, or whether they are read from a place of profound loss and sadness, they are the foundation for this entire book. When the last word is read, the last page turned, and the book closed, it comes down to this: Do we believe that we are God's first? Are we held by God always, in all the wonderful and awful times of our lives? Do we recognize and honor daily that the other half of the marriage or union is in God's hands as well? Are we willing to give our common lives over to God, trusting that grace will mark our days? If the covenant relationship is broken, do we trust that we will still remain in God's love? It is much easier to talk about the myriad factors of a life situation than it is about the underpinnings that support it all. It is also much easier to see in the myriad factors of a life situation the possibilities for an abundant life if the underpinnings are known and valued. This chapter is not about specific actions as much as it is about the well of love and strength that can infuse those actions in everyday life. Courage is needed and trustworthiness a must if the lives of both partners are to be lived in faith—not at each other's expense, but because of each other's willing sacrifice.

FEAR NOT!

> The LORD is my light and my salvation; whom shall I fear?
> The LORD is the stronghold of my life: of whom shall I be afraid?
> (Psa. 27:1)

> There is no fear in love, but perfect love casts out fear; for fear has to do with punishment, and whoever fears has not reached perfection in love. We love because he first loved us. (1 John 4:18–19)

Holy ground is a scary patch of real estate. It's no wonder that the first thing most people do when they encounter God is drop to the ground, face in the dirt. It is a miraculous sign of God's love that the first words most people hear from their encounter with the Divine is some version of "fear not!"[1] Coming into the presence of holiness, walking into sacred space, traveling across sacred ground requires courage and a reassuring word from God that there is no reason to fear.

No one is perfect, not in action or thought. No one will act in perfect love, or be able to let go of all fear. Fear of loss, of betrayal, and of loneliness haunt most everyone to one degree or another. People get hurt by those they love. Spouses and partners of the ordained or nonordained variety will disappoint their other halves, and forgiveness is needed when this happens. But the fear of hurt and betrayal, the fear of taking the risk of living in a deep covenantal relationship, is not the same as the fear one feels when walking on holy ground. Fear of holy ground is the very human and very appropriate response to being in God's presence. It is fear that is born of awe. The fear in this is not that the sacred ground will give way, but that the holiness of it all is just too much to contain in one human life. This is the fear of overwhelming love, and the graciousness of the God who offers it to us in ways that lead us to life rather than death.

Fear of God, the awe all people feel when God shows up in their lives, is a gift. It is a difficult one to receive: many people who have had a remarkable encounter with God are thankful for it but do not ask to have another! This fear of holy ground, of the sacred encounter, is natural because everyone realizes his or her own imperfection when confronted with God's perfect love. But this is not shaming, or something that destroys: this absolute knowledge of one's own imperfect nature takes place in the eternal love and acceptance of God's presence. God's delight surrounds the encounter and overtakes the acute awareness of imperfection and unworthiness. The truth is that no one is worthy of God's love and attention, but everyone is guaranteed that same love and attention. It is a gift to be created by God and held by God, and it makes one's shortcomings a paltry matter not worth obsessing over. It may also allow a person to accept the imperfections of another with graciousness, secure in the knowledge that God loves both equally. Even with spouses and partners, perhaps especially with spouses and partners, the gift of God's love freely given and acceptance of shortcomings brings strength and forgiveness into the very fiber of the relationship.

As overwhelming as God's presence is, it is not something that is foisted upon the unwilling. God is gracious and will wait for an invitation to enter the lives of individuals, couples, families, and communities. God does not remove the right to refuse communion from anyone, so permission to enter is required. This does not mean that a couple must say "Come on in, God," or do anything so obvious. The invitation can be there on a level deeper than conscious awareness. It is the openness to God that allows one to be scared to life rather than scared to death. When one offers all the joys and sorrows of life to God, God will take that gift. It isn't taken away forever, but returned in a new way. Transformed by the love of God, it is handed back in a way that deepens faith and brings great joy. This joy goes beyond the individual, infusing all the important relationships of that person's life. It brings about change, for nothing touched by God maintains its old form and meaning.

What happens to a spouse or partner when a life offered to God by the other half is returned in a new configuration? Whether it is the ordained half or the lay half, it has a profound effect upon the relationship.

Things must change because God has given a gift to that couple. But such a sacred gift does not come without responsibility. Both partners must honor that, incorporating it into their relationship. It goes beyond the couple, too. When shared with family, friends, and the larger faith community, it becomes an instance of grace for the world. Just as a terrible tragedy can devastate an entire community, so a wonderful good can heal relationships and hurts far beyond the individual or couple who share in it. Such good can lead to an abundance of life that is as extraordinary as it is tangible.

ABUNDANT LIFE

"The thief comes only to steal and kill and destroy. I came that they may have life, and have it more abundantly" (John 10:10).

Jesus speaks these words in the Gospel of John, trying to help his disciples understand who he is. In the verses before and after this one, Jesus calls himself the *good shepherd,* the one who cares for his flock and lives so that they may have abundant life themselves. But what does abundant life look like? How is an abundant life in covenant relationship lived with an ordained ministry an integral element? Each couple and each individual will have a unique take on abundance, for every person is unique and will live into abundance in original ways. Still, there are some common elements that make it easier to live a life full of grace—an abundant life offered in Christ.

Presence of Love, Not Just Absence of Malice

Abundant life is not a neutral backdrop for life's comings and goings; it is a powerful and living reality. It requires active and intentional loving to sustain it. This kind of love is not movie romantic love, although romance can be a door to sustaining love. This love is not an accident of time and place or hormones and moonlight, but the positive presence that comes from daily commitment and choice. It is not just the absence of dislike or ill intention, but the presence of meaning good things for each other. This love is not just choosing against hurting someone, it is a vigorous choosing to foster the life of the other. It involves sacrifice and must take into consideration all members of the family. It is the kind of love Paul writes of in his first letter to the church at Corinth, the words so often read at weddings and so rarely taken seriously (1 Cor. 13).

This kind of love involves sacrifices from both covenant partners. It isn't easy to sustain, but it is life-sustaining for both. It is one of the ways that God blesses marriages and unions. The presence of love frames the lives of the couple in a unique and flexible way. Sacrifices are made for the other; opportunities are not pursued to the exclusion of the other. Everyone in covenant relationship will give up certain paths and individual pursuits to foster a partner's life and to foster their relationship. This giving up is not at the expense of the other person if there is a vital love present because the giving up is shared. When sacrifice turns into one partner's gain at the expense of the other, when mutuality is not part of the couple's reality, love's tangible presence will evaporate. For an abundant life, this presence is necessary. With the difficulties facing spouses and partners, this sustaining love can be a lifeline.

Presence of Sabbath Rest

Sabbath rest, the time to play and pray together, is vital to living an abundant life. It gives the couple a time to orient their lives toward the God who created them and now sustains them. It also provides the environment for the couple to join their lives together in tangible ways every week. Sabbath rest, with its play and pray time, helps clear away the distracting elements of life that put distance between the covenant partners. Sabbath is the pause, the time to breathe slowly and give the world back to God. No one is cut out to be Atlas, bearing the weight of the world. Sabbath keeps a couple from missing out on the biggest truth: everything belongs to God. Most people need an ongoing, consistent time to live into that truth. Sabbath promotes living into our true selves, letting our partners be their true selves, and freeing our children and friends to be who they are: God's beloved.

Trust

Trust is vital, but so difficult to include as foundational to an abundant life. Trust is not an individual achievement, but something done in the company of others. For a couple, trust means risking individual well-being and security for connection. One partner cannot force the other to be trustworthy. One partner can only remain open to the other, giving his or her other half the gift of a common life. This is not just a commonality of location or activity, but a commonality of vulnerability. Trust requires that each individual give up a back-up plan, an easy exit in case things "don't work out." Hedging bets may be the prudent and safe thing to do, especially with separation and divorce so available.[2] Trust answers with a yes the question "will we stand together and support each other when life is at its most difficult?" Trust is relying on the constancy and respect of the other so that both can grow as a couple and as individuals. When each person answers "will you be here?" with a "yes," trust grows.

What if things fall apart? What if one person in the relationship breaks trust? This is the negation of trust, and it inflicts deep wounds. When the trust of one is betrayed by the other, every facet of life is wounded. Taking the chance to be open and in relationship is taking a chance because there are no guarantees. One partner can be betrayed by the other. One partner who never thought it possible may betray his or her other half for a variety of reasons. No one is perfect, and everyone has the power to inflict pain on his or her spouse. Trust is not something that can be done by one individual for another, but something that depends upon the love, care, and honesty of both. When it is violated, deep pain results. For some, the risk of that pain precludes trust in the first place. For others, there is no second chance to trust once it has been broken. For still others, trust may come again. The way back is painful and long, but with forgiveness and humor, and the awareness that God will not abandon anyone, the journey can be made back to covenant and forward to an abundant reality.

It is important to make a distinction between broken trust and an abusive relationship. If one partner is abused in any way, he or she should not return to that relationship. Returning will not end the abuse and may lead to irreparable damage, even to death.

Trust or its absence affects every aspect of life for a couple. Trust brings the freedom to let the partners go out into the world to work and enjoy life without suspicion. Lack of trust brings anxiety every time one or both partners are out of the house. The amount of time and energy it takes to prove or disprove suspicions is considerable, and robs the couple of the ability to move together toward abundance. Trust frees a couple to assume the care and concern of each for the other, not in a way that discounts it, but in a way that allows their focus and energy to go toward the creation of an abundant life rather than toward the defense against a damaging one. The stakes are high, and it is a gamble. Yet God is constant and will hold each person fast, even when trust is broken.

PRISCILLA AND AQUILA—ABUNDANT LIFE IN CONNECTED WORK

What brings abundance into one couple's life may be quite different than what nourishes another. Much depends upon the individuals involved, and on how they relate their baptismal ministries and an ordained calling. Are they coworkers in a joint ministry, or are their work lives separate? What goes into living an abundant life in light of a full time ordained ministry?

For those who see their lives joined not only by a marriage or union but by a joint ministry, Priscilla and Aquila provide a biblical example. This wife and husband team worked with the apostle Paul, traveling to spread the good news of Jesus Christ while working together in the tent making profession. They were connected by common faith, common service, and a common private life. While most couples are connected by their home life and larger circle of friends and family, few today work side by side at a common task or calling. For those who do, for the couples who join their calls to serve Christ in the world, there can be an extraordinary bond. They share dreams and worries about the same work life, the same family life, and the same faith community. Whether one or both are ordained, the ministry is held in common. As long as each considers the other equal before God, the division of tasks and the perceptions of inequality from the outside world will not cause damage. Each partner has the opportunity to see how the other half shows love to the world through work. What a gift that is, and it brings a deep level of appreciation for both. Life is rich.

In professional relationships in almost every field and workplace, competition is a decisive factor. Coworkers strive for advancement by working to be the best at their profession, and often by besting each other through their work. There are limited numbers of promotions, creating an atmosphere in which one person's promotion is another's loss. This dog-eat-dog approach can be damaging to coworkers whose lives are not connected outside the workplace, but can be devastating to partners who work together. When one partner competes with the other, their joint work becomes the field for their individual wins and losses. Each person is trying to defeat the competition. When joint ministry and common work become grounds for competition rather than mutuality in ministerial tasks, someone wins and someone loses. In a professional situation that involves one ordained half and a lay half, it's not difficult to see who is going to lose that competition. For joint ministry and a personal relationship to bring more abundance into the couple's life, competition must be given up. Neither wins anything if their common ministry and common life reduce both to winners and losers. Defeated are the individuals, their covenant, and their service to God in the world.

For a couple who works together, comparisons in style and ability are inevitable. The faith community at large may very well value the work of one over the other. This is especially true and quite natural if only one partner is ordained. The work of the lay spouse, even if done as a paid employee, will be seen as secondary to the work of the ordained half. To survive this, a foundational sense of equality must be maintained by the couple. When one half of the couple feels like a lesser version of the other, no amount of outward success will bring a sense of God's abundance. When one seeks to be greater than the other by besting him or her through work, the abundant life is thrown away. Each partner stands equal before God, and both should see the other as his or her equal in the most profound sense. Particular abilities and public recognition cannot make one person more or less valuable than another unless the couple allows it.

When the two partners refuse to compete against each other, when neither considers himself or herself of greater or lesser value than the other, their common life is strengthened through their mutual work. It is a marvelous gift to witness how a partner's baptismal ministry is lived through work. The spouse who sees his or her other half's service to Christ in the world gains a deep appreciation for the gifts given to enrich the world. The unique abilities and qualities of both are celebrated and enhanced by the other. In this greater appreciation, both partners come closer to seeing God's image more clearly in each other's lives. Mutual gratitude frees the couple to delight in their individuality and in their union. The years of common life and work become the story of reciprocal respect and thankfulness. What an extraordinary way to live life!

The last element for the Priscilla and Aquila couples who work together is a clear sense of perspective. It is crucial for both to remember and live into the absolute truth that their professional identities and their professional working relationship are secondary. Their primary identities are secure in being God's beloved. Their working relationship, whatever its outward equality or inequality, is enveloped in their fundamental equality before God and in the equality of their service to God. There is no winner and no loser, only two people bound in love and held by God. With no energy or intention wasted upon besting one another, both are freed to live an abundant life together.

DEBORAH AND LAPPIDOTH—ABUNDANT LIFE IN DIFFERENT DIRECTIONS

Unlike Priscilla and Aquila, Lappidoth and Deborah did not share a common work life. There is no record of Lappidoth joining Deborah as she served as judge, or as she went to war. Their only connection was in their personal relationship. Whatever Lappidoth did for work is not recorded, but it most likely involved a different context than Deborah's work. He was not called to be a judge, to render judgments on political, legal, and religious matters. His work was in a different direction. This is the situation that most partners and their clergy others find themselves in. What elements lead to an abundant life in this work configuration?

The working lives of both partners take a lot of time and energy. This is true when there are two careers pursued and when one partner concentrates on running the home and volunteer work, and for those working only part-time. Maintaining a life is hard work, however many paychecks are involved. How each covenant partner sees this time and energy spent elsewhere makes a big difference when seeking an abundant life. Is the time away seen as unrelated to the union, or understood as something that can enrich it? Do the two divide in the morning to go out and conquer their unconnected work worlds, or do they set out on separate journeys and return to share their adventures? When the time and effort that go into any work are seen as something totally removed from the relationship, a lot of meaningful sharing can be forfeited. "How was your day, dear?" becomes a perfunctory question rather than the beginning of a conversation that can connect the work world to the couple's common life.[3] If work time is a time to go out and battle the world, then it is tempting to view the off time at home as recovery time rather than time to reconnect. Work as a battle is something negative to the relationship, something that should remain outside the private sphere. This results in a great chunk of time and effort being lost as an opportunity to grow closer.

When the working lives of both partners are seen as temporary journeys in different directions, then relating the events of the day becomes a sharing of two adventures. This does not mean that something amazing must happen each and every day, but that both partners have the chance to experience how the other half lives during the hours apart. Both come back to share their adventures, providing glimpses into another way to live in the world. Both listen actively as the day's events are recounted because they value each other's time and efforts. For the one recounting his or her day, the partner provides a sounding board, a concerned listener who can see in the minutiae of daily work a significance that is often lost on the one doing it. For the listening partner, the other's tales of the day bring an opportunity to enjoy a different perspective and the chance to ask questions. Why did he remember this particular event? What does her retelling of the day reveal about her values? Why did he find that particular slogan amusing? Why did she find something meaningful that most people didn't even notice? How do daily adventures and their retelling bless both with glimpses into each other's souls? Framing work life as a journey or adventure to be shared with a partner or spouse brings the opportunity to appreciate the unique perspective that each brings to the relationship. Sharing the joys and concerns that arise at work can help both spouses see their significant other as more than an extension of themselves: the other becomes more unique in his or her partner's eyes at the same time as he or she is more deeply connected by the experiences they share at the end of the day. It is much more difficult to take the other for granted when his or her work life is valued as part of their commonly held story and as a gift to the wider world. Lappidoth does not have to be at the battles with Deborah for those battles to become part of the story that is their common life. Deborah does not have to lose the time she spent at work because Lappidoth's retelling of his time gives it to her. A view from the other half is the unique opportunity to be enriched by the other's life experience—a blessing gained by listening actively and appreciating the adventures of the other half.

When the lay and ordained partners do not spend their work hours together, they do not see the other's public work persona. The professional identities of both may be dropped upon entering the home as both resume their private and related identities as people in covenant relationship. What the couple can see in each other is how the public face, the work persona, affects the person underneath it. Does the working self enrich the one working, or drain away precious energy? Are the working selves natural extensions of the persons inside them or in opposition to them? Do the work lives of both partners suck the life out of them or add another blessing to the lives they live? These questions are important, and answering them can help both partners see the effects of work on their overall lives. A spouse can be the first to see the benefits of the other's working life, and may be the firsthand witness to the damage done by it. This is true for both, not just for the ordained partner. Any kind of work can be draining, and most work can lead to greater satisfaction and abundance.

A partner can help keep his or her other half real. When the work life of one is taking a toll on the inner person and the shared relationship, a spouse can pay attention to it. If the work or how the work is done taxes more than invigorates, then change may be necessary. Partners can help each other by raising questions when the private person and the person at work do not relate. If the work persona becomes a façade constructed to get through the day, then it will drain the life of the individual and the couple's common life. When a caring other questions soul-killing work practices, and when such concerns are taken seriously, an abundant life is fostered. If the concerns are disregarded, the common life loses a marvelous opportunity to grow.

When a couple live in the Deborah and Lappidoth work reality, mutual respect and interest in each other's work is a must. Neither one is going to know everything that goes into the other's job; neither one will experience the ongoing demands, rewards, and drawbacks to the other's position. There will be things too inconsequential to relate, issues of confidentiality that bar sharing, and a lot of effort that will go unnoticed by the spouse. It is easy to stop asking about the other's work life, and it takes no thought to lose sight of the importance that working life has for the other. Mutual appreciation comes by taking the time to learn about the other's work. What makes the work so interesting to him or her? What elements of work are difficult or tedious? Is the partner happy with his or her working life? Are his or her gifts being used in a way that makes the world a better place? What value does the partner put on work? Seeking the answers to these questions shows respect for the other's working life. It takes time, energy, and focused attention to value the work of a partner, but it is worth every effort. Both have the opportunity to see how the individual who is their partner adds something to the world beyond the couple's home. By maintaining an interest in each other's work, both have the opportunity to remember and experience why their other half was so appealing to begin with.

Do partners and spouses need to know every little thing about the other's daily work? No. But both should have an informed understanding of what their other half does. If these questions can be answered, chances are that the partners are appreciative of the work of their other half:

- What is my partner's official title? What is his or her work phone number and extension?
- What does my spouse do in his or her daily work? Does he or she enjoy the work environment?
- Who works closely with my partner? If my spouse works alone, what does he or she do?
- What is new in my spouse's work life in the past two weeks? What are the ongoing projects?
- Are there stressful situations at work? If asked, can I say what my partner's work life is like?
- Have I told my spouse that I appreciate his or her work?

Many of these questions relate to the issues brought up in chapter 3 but are worth a second look. When both partners show respect for the work of the other, their relationship is enriched. When both partners take time to learn of the other's work, they give the gift of care and concern to the other. That care and concern lead to a life of greater abundance.

There should be an eleventh commandment for couples whose working lives are not held in common: Thou shalt not covet thy partner's job, abilities, gifts, and opportunities. It is an easy thing to let jealousy creep into a relationship, especially if the larger community considers one partner's work worth more than the work of the other. Because ordained ministry is often considered a "higher" calling than other careers, it is easy for the nonordained half to feel that his or her work is undervalued or less valuable. But this judgment, even if it is made by the world beyond the couple's relationship, has no place within their common life. The work of one should not be considered more valuable, just as the worth of one is no more than the other. When one or both of the spouses relegates one person's work to second-class status, it can very easily lead to feelings of inadequacy. No person's worth is reduced to the work of his or her hands, and neither partner should feel that the other's work devalues his or her own work. For an abundant life, both spouses must seek each other's well-being and each other's companionship. They should not be competing with each other to win "the most important work" award. Being happy for the other and refusing to compete with the other moves the careers of both out of competition mode and into a framework of mutual respect. The value and appreciation that the two covenant partners have for their own work and the work of the other can bless their common life in ways far beyond financial gain and professional prestige.

STILL TOGETHER, FOLLOWING JESUS

When Jesus calls the disciples to follow him, they leave boats and nets behind to begin their new journey of faith. When a couple unites to follow Jesus together, they embark on a new journey of faith. This is not a quick trip to the city for the weekend, or an occasional foray into the world, but a long and wonderful trek. They have each other as companions on the way, and they have the wider community of faith accompanying them. What they do not have is an end destination in sight. This is the trip of a lifetime, and it will be the shared adventure of the couple's lifetime, bringing opportunities for each to discern a ministry and to work out the details of it alongside another. Along the way, children and careers add depth and complication to it all. Many things prayed for will arrive, bringing with them additional responsibility. How can the couple manage to hold on to each other, to continue walking the road together, when all these other things are coming along, too?

One way to stay connected and to live into an abundant life is to pay attention to dreams. What dreams are shared by the couple? What dreams does one partner have for the other? What dreams does a spouse have for the couple's children? What do they pray for as a couple, as individuals for themselves, and as individuals praying for their covenant partner? Where do their separate dreams touch? Are these dreams for self, other, family, friends, community, and world shared with the other half? Do both of the partners appreciate the dreams of the other, incorporating them into individual prayers and hopes? Dreams are delicate strands that connect the present to the future that is in the making. When both dream for their partners good things in this world and on this journey of faith, wonderful things can happen. When both honor the other by taking their dreams seriously and seeking to bring those dreams to faithful fruition, the world itself is transformed. Each partner sees the other half as a marvelous, complex, and blessed companion throughout life. This deepens love and binds the couple more willingly and strongly together.

For many couples, sharing dreams and dreaming for each other are not part of their common life. Some don't think about it, others don't value it. Still others lack the courage to dream dreams for themselves and those they love. What if dreams do not come true? What if one is brave enough and willing enough to dream, but the other is not? Perhaps some feel that it is better not to dream for the self and a partner if those dreams don't come with a guarantee. It takes an open spirit and a generous heart to dream. It takes a lot of faith to make dreaming an integral part of a couple's faith journey together, but it is worth the effort.

Certain things make dreaming, sharing dreams, and working toward them difficult. Old grievances never addressed sap the ability to see in the future something marvelous for the self and the other half. Lack of time and interest in the daily life of the other squash dreams as well. Living daily life without valuing one's own self keeps dreams away. When there is too much stress and not enough rest, dreaming dreams of faith together becomes nearly impossible. Dreams are not free: they require time and attention and a spirit open to new possibilities. But dreams can help a couple see that the ways to serve God are many, and that there is great hope in the service. If one partner cannot dream good things for his or her partner, when the dreams of the self and other are considered worthless, a couple should ask this question: what must be let go of to dream dreams again? The couple must also be willing to change their relationship in light of the answer. God has created an infinitely interesting and complex world: is it any wonder that dreams can come true?

GIVING OURSELVES BACK TO GOD

Most of our waking hours seem to be spent giving time and energy to various causes and people. Children and work, spouses and friends, and the wider world ask for attention and labor. Most spend a lifetime trying to construct a fruitful reality for self and for those they love. But does that lead to an abundant life?

It is part of faith reality that what fosters the spiritual life is not necessarily self-promoting. When a person makes his or her individual goals and aspirations the center of everything he or she does, much that leads to peace is left behind. For a couple in covenant relationship, neither can be the center of everything because that makes the partner's life secondary. Neither can the couple's relationship be the center of reality, for they do not fully create their own reality or the reality of others. The world was not created for the benefit and use of one particular person or couple, or community, for that matter. The world was created by God, and God declared it good long before anyone living today took a first breath. It is giving the self and the other half back to God that brings a couple into the largest perspective possible: the vantage point that reveals that God holds everyone and everything fast. This is not the usual perspective, for it involves considering others as equal to self. It also confronts all people with the hard fact that no single person created his or her own reality, and no person can dictate how the entire reality of the world should be understood.

To believe that reality at its most loving and profound is not a creation of any one person, couple, or group of people is to affirm the most profound and loving truth of all: that God sets the context in which all life is lived and fostered. Instead of God being an object in human reality, no matter how big or beloved, this true perspective reveals that humans are beloved creatures in God's reality. It is the reverse of how most humans understand their lives, for doesn't everyone live life from their own perspective? When the single perspective is given over to God in the hopes of living into a much larger reality, then a truly holy vision can be revealed. The primary pursuit from this place is not the working out of the individual's or couple's dreams for themselves and for others. The primary question is this: What are God's dreams for us?

What does God dream about for every person? What dreams does God have for children, a partner or spouse, for self, and for the beautiful world beyond the family? No one can fully grasp the mind of God, and God's thoughts and dreams are beyond human comprehension as a whole. Still, these dreams can be sought in prayer, most especially when dreams are handed over to God in faith. We seek to know not only God's thoughts on the activities and decisions of our lives, but to know God's hopes for the dreams that will come. This is not projecting our particular aspirations into God's mind, making our own wishes seemingly divine; this is offering our most cherished hopes to God and being drawn into God's world in the process. Our dreams are returned eventually, most likely in a different form. They become ways of walking on holy ground rather than yardsticks of comparison to the work or dreams of others.

This talk of dreams may seem flighty to some, not substantial or helpful for living daily life. But dreams and prayers offered to God bring meaning into daily life in a way that nothing else can. If Jesus' presence in the world and Jesus' care for the troubles of others reveal anything, it is this: we are most firmly planted in the real world when we stand in God's world. Jesus participated in human life; he did not remove himself or his followers from it. When we seek God's dreams for ourselves and others, we are not removed from our particular circumstances—we are planted more firmly in them because we see them from a larger perspective. But what does this mean for spouses or partner and an ordained half?

SEEING GOD'S GRACE IN OUR SPOUSES AND PARTNERS

When the dreams a couple dreams are given to God in trust, it fosters a deeper appreciation for the immeasurable worth of both partners. God's grace is visible not only in the life of one of the partners, but in the lives of both. Equality in God's eyes is the promise that our spouse or partner is a child of God. Letting him or her be the child that God loves, fosters, and sustains makes it much more difficult to take him or her for granted. No one was put on this earth merely to be the spouse or partner of another person. God delights in each person as is, not only because he or she is joined to another. Marriage or union is the chosen way that both live out their faith lives, but it is not the sole reason for the life of either.

When we accept our partner or spouse as belonging to God first, we accept ourselves in the same way. We let ourselves be children of God first, not people who perform specific tasks or live in relationship to particular people. Marriage or union does not dissolve the unique nature of any person; it merely places it in a different context. Marriage or union is not the ultimate ground of anyone's identity—God is. When our marriages and unions are seen as resting in God's hands, we allow ourselves to grow more and more into the blessed life God intends for us and dreams for us. We can let go of a functional view of ourselves and our partners. It is not about who does what for the other, or who has the highest score in the game of marriage. God delights in us as individuals and as a couple. We honor that delight and live into it more deeply by honoring each other. The two in covenant relationship are a community of faith. When both partners honor their other half and themselves as God's, a precious gift of grace enters the world.

SEEKING DEEPER RELATIONSHIPS WITH FAMILY, HELD IN GOD'S LOVE

No one's life is completely encompassed by work. A great deal of life happens beyond the work hours and location. The life of the family is something that is not a job, but the context in which we live and grow. This includes the families we are born into, the families we gain through marriage or union, and the families of loved ones who make up the wider circle of friends. When time, attention, and energy are devoted to deepening loving family relationships, everyone is made richer. But to do this well, both the partner and clergy half must step out of work mode. The work of the couple is important and can lead to a richer life, but only if set in the larger context of relationship to God and others. When a spouse moves into the world outside of work, he or she can more clearly see the value of that work. The sense of self is expanded because the very real danger of reducing personal worth to work identity and productivity is overcome. Because friends and family appreciate the partner as a person rather than as someone producing a particular product, a greater sense of the self as intrinsically valuable emerges. This intrinsic value is the gift of being God's first, and can be constantly affirmed when life is seen as more than a series of workdays.

Most adults have multiple roles in life. They are partners, parents, children, friends, employers and employees, volunteers for causes, caregivers, cooks, homeowners or renters, and cleaners. In any one day, several of these roles come into play. Sometimes all the roles work well together, leading to a high degree of satisfaction. Sometimes the roles conflict, with one or more requiring too much time and effort to be satisfying. Life can become a series of tasks to perform, a succession of hurdles to jump. When one role takes the majority of time and effort, it is easy for it to become the defining role. When ordained ministry is one of the roles, it is too easy for it to become all-consuming. When this happens, both partners lose sight of the value of everything else. This can be true of any profession, but is a very real issue in fields that involve caring for other people. Doctors, social workers, therapists, and teachers face a similar situation, but not necessarily with the added ingredient of faith.

When the various roles that both partners fill are understood as necessary and important partial identities, it becomes easier for both to let go of them. Both may wear many hats but cling less tightly to any individual one because who they are as individuals and as a couple is not defined exclusively by one role. A single role can be life enriching, but it cannot and should not be life defining. True identity resides in God's delight rather than in a particular role, and each role can be picked up or set aside when necessary. Ironically, this ability to take even important roles less seriously often leads to greater ability and fulfillment in those roles. The stakes are lower because personal identity and value are beyond the parameters of the individual roles, and beyond their collective reality. This kind of perspective allows a spouse and clergy half to view their work as something that can be changed, questioned, and fully appreciated. Neither must lose their soul to the work of their hands.

As partners in marriage or union, the two live together in an ever changing, living relationship. As each grows older and experiences new things,

partner's ability and willingness to accept a less than perfect other half, and trust that God delights in the honest, imperfect, created self. With practice, the true self can emerge from behind the created shell. With trust in God, each individual can allow his or her true self to emerge. This self is more vulnerable to the inevitable hurts that come from living with other imperfect humans, but it is also more capable of recovering from those hurts. Nothing can remove God's constant love.

No individual is perfect. Everyone has faults and everyone makes mistakes. Because no one is perfect, no two are perfect together. There is no such thing as a perfect relationship or a perfect partner. It is absolutely true that it is easier for some couples to live in fruitful covenant than for others. But each covenant relationship will face difficulties. Both partners will disappoint and be disappointed in each other. It is what they do that determines whether their common life is fostered or allowed to die.

The ties that bind a covenant couple together are real. Neither partner can disregard those ties, for they are not free to pursue life in isolation from the other half. For some, such ties become fetters. The bond becomes something that chafes rather than supports. If one or both of the partners cannot give up an isolated sense of individuality in favor of an individuality that grows in relationship, life can become a series of negotiations for individual rights.

When a couple sees the ties that bind them together as the gift of positive connection, those ties become the material from which their common life is woven. The sacrifices that one makes for the other are not harmful because they lead to a greater sense of individuality and a deeper connection. The sense of self is deepened along with the sense of the partner. Self-giving expands the self, and allows the beloved partner's self to grow. Care for self and care for the partner are not in opposition but work together to create a wonderfully complex and enriching common life.

What happens when the ties that bind are broken? That is the dangerous question, and the one that prevents many couples from living a deep common life. Imperfect people make mistakes. They hurt themselves and those they love. They break promises and they seek their own good at the expense of others. The stresses that ordained ministry places on a marriage or union are very real, and sometimes sap the energy of both partners to the point that the common life is strained. It is safer for both to hold back a part of who they are from their covenant. That one part is held in reserve in case things break. While only full commitment to the covenant can lead to a deeply abundant life together, partial commitment can provide a functional relationship. A functional relationship may be easier to leave when things go awry, but it is never as deep or as satisfying as a fully committed one.

Life for the spouses and partners of ministers is risky because the complexities of clergy life require a lot of personal energy and attention. If the minister cannot reserve enough of his or her life for a partner, the partner is left with no companion for life's journey. It often falls to the spouse to sound the alarm when ministry threatens the covenant promises, or when the faith life of the nonordained half is suffering. It takes diligence to maintain a relationship with a partner, and it takes sacrifice and integrity to do it alongside an ordained ministry. These very complexities that make it difficult are also the very things that make it rich. It is up to the couple to decide: will we seek an abundant covenant life while working out our faith together, or will we choose another path? In either case, God will hold all things fast.

BENEDICTION

So how should this voyage end? What is the final word for a book about the lives of clergy spouses and partners? At this ending, only a benediction will do. After worship, the faith community is sent out into their daily lives with wishes for a good life. A benediction is a wishing well, a blessing for the time between communal worship.

This book is in no way a communal worship, but it is a reflection on the life issues that many clergy spouses and partners have in common. It is a gathering of situations, of possibilities, of difficulties, and of information. The words and topics in these pages were inspired by the many spouses and partners who shared their struggles and joys. The quotes and concrete situations are gifts from partners and spouses kind enough to share their experiences directly. In that way, one could imagine that this book is a window that reveals a spouse and partner community. For the spouses and partners who informed this book and for the ones who read it; for the ordained halves of the covenant; for concerned others who have taken the time to read this collection of words and thoughts:

The grace of God,
deeper than our imagination;
the strength of Christ,
stronger than our need;
and the communion of the Holy Spirit,
richer than our togetherness
guide and sustain us today
and in all our tomorrows.[4]

Amen. (So be it! Let it be!)

APPENDIX A

Survey for Clergy Spouses and Partners

Name (optional): ______________________________

Gender (circle): male female

Age (circle): 18–22 23–30 31–45 46–60 61–70 71–80 81+

Children (circle): yes no

Number of children: ______________________________

Ages of children: ______________________________

Years married /committed relationship: ______________________________

Your faith tradition, if any: ______________________________

Is your faith important in your life? Why or why not?

Do you and your spouse practice the same religion? If yes, do you belong to the same denomination or tradition of faith?

Did you know going into marriage/committed relationship that you were going to be a clergy spouse/partner?

As a child, were you part of a clergy family?

Are you a two-career family? If yes, do you need to work for financial reasons? If yes, would you work if you did not need to? Why?

Do you feel pressure to participate in the ministry of your spouse/partner's church?

What is your perception of the support that you receive (circle location on each line)?

	(strong) ←			→ *(weak)*	
SPOUSE/PARTNER	5	4	3	2	1
CHURCH	5	4	3	2	1
WORK	5	4	3	2	1
FAMILY	5	4	3	2	1
FRIENDS/COMMUNITY	5	4	3	2	1

Clarify/Explain:

Do you live in church-owned housing (parsonage, rectory, manse)? If yes, is this advantageous or not?

Do you invite members of your faith community into your home?

If yes, has it been a positive experience, negative, mixed?

Do you and your spouse keep a Sabbath? If yes, how? If no, comments?

Are you called to a particular vocation? Is this a secular or church call?

Did you have any input into your spouse's/partner's decision to seek ministry or in the context of her/his call?

Should a call be accepted without the agreement of both you and your spouse/partner?

Have you started any family traditions since being in the ministry?

Have your holiday traditions changed since being in the ministry? Can you give an example?

Whom do you seek out in times of crisis?

Can your spouse/partner be your minister? Please explain.

Does your spouse/partner have detailed knowledge of your work?

Does he/she believe it is important? If so, how is it demonstrated?

Who has the primary responsibility for your children's faith upbringing?

Are they involved in your spouse's/partner's faith community?

Does professional ministry infringe upon your family time? Please explain or give an example.

Do you have close friends outside of your faith community? Local or far away?

How do you nurture and maintain these friendships?

How much time a week to you devote to your personal faith?

Do you experience significant conflict with your spouse/partner? If yes, how do you cope with it?

Would you handle it differently if you were not a clergy spouse/partner?

Are there thoughts you feel important for us to know concerning life as a clergy partner or spouse? Feel free to write on the back of this paper.

Thank you for completing this survey. Your participation is appreciated. If you have any questions, you may contact me at clergyspouseproject@gmail.com. Please return this survey in the envelope provided.

APPENDIX B

Survey Consent Form

March, 2009

Dear Participant:

There is ongoing research on the subject of the quality of life of clergymen and clergywomen but very little research on the quality of life of their spouses and partners. This survey is a way to gather information about the lives of clergy spouses and partners. It is part of a larger project to define the issues facing partners and spouses in order to serve their needs more adequately. Because there is very little information concerning clergy partners and spouses, your participation in this survey is very important. The survey can be completed in ten minutes. Depending upon how many comments you choose to include, it may take longer. Please feel free to spend as much or as little time on this as you like.

The information gathered through this survey is confidential. The comments will be used to deepen understanding and illustrate issues facing clergy spouses and partners. No names or locations of respondents will be revealed. By signing this consent form, you give permission to use your comments.

Your time and effort are a necessary part of this project and are appreciated. If you have any questions or comments concerning this survey, you may contact me at clergyspouseproject@gmail.com. Thank you for your participation.

Johnna Fredrickson, PhD

CONSENT FORM

I, ______________________________, give permission for my comments to be used in the ongoing clergy spouse and partner research project. My answers and comments will be used only for this purpose and my participation will remain confidential.

Signature ______________________________

Date __________________________________

NOTES

Introductory Words

1. "Christian Marriage Rite I," 843. From *Book of Common Worship* © 1993 Westminster John Knox Press. Used by permission.

2. Ibid., 844–45.

3. *The Book of Common Prayer*, according to the use of the Episcopal Church (New York: Oxford University Press, 1990), 429–30. These prayers are common to many marriage rites within the Christian faith.

4. David R. Anderson, "Wreckonciliation," *Tidings*, newsletter of St. Luke's Parish, Episcopal Church (U.S.A). Darien, Conn. (February 26, 2006). Reprinted in the March edition with Pam Anderson's reply.

5. "Memo: 'Wreckonciliation,'" *Tidings* (March 26, 2006): 12.

Chapter One

1. From "The Baptismal Covenant," *The Book of Common Prayer*, 306–8.

2. From "The Sacrament of Baptism," *Book of Common Worship*, 405–14. List adapted from the Presbyterian Church (U.S.A.) website, http://pcusa.org. from

3. Commission on Ministry, *Ordination Discernment Handbook 2006* (Episcopal Diocese of Massachusetts, 2006), 3.

4. Richard M. Webster, Project Director, Presbyterian Church (U.S.A.), "Primary Qualities for Professional Ministry," SEIC Resource #92-102, 1, http://www.pcusa.org/prep4min/pdf/primary_qualities.pdf, accessed May 20,2010.

5. From Episcopal Diocese of Massachusetts Commission on Ministry, *2010 Discernment for Ministry: A Handbook for The Episcopal Diocese of Massachusetts*, http://www.diomass.org/webfm_send/1538.

6. UCC Ministry Issues Implementation Committee, "The Marks of Faithful and Effective Authorized Ministers of the United Church of Christ," excerpts from *Implementing the Pronouncement: Ministry Issues: Forming and Preparing Pastoral Leaders for God's Church*, 13–21, draft 3.1, April 2009, www.ucc.org/ministers/pdfs/Marks-of-Faithful-and-Effective-Authorized-Ministers.pdf, 7.

7. Ibid., 5.

8. Episcopal Diocese of Massachusetts Commission on Ministry, *2010 Discernment for Ministry, 16.*

9. Webster, "Primary Qualities for Professional Ministry," 4.

10. Similar accounts can be found in Mark 1:16–20, Luke 5:1–11, and John 1:35–51.

11. Douglas R. A. Hare, "Matthew," in *Interpretation: A Biblical Commentary for Teaching and Preaching* (Louisville: John Knox Press, 1993), 30.

12. M. O'Connor, "Judges," in *The New Jerome Biblical Commentary* (Englewood Cliffs, N.J.: Prentice Hall, 1990), 133.

13. William H. Willimon, "Acts," in *Interpretation Series* (Louisville: John Knox Press, 1998), 145.

14. Not all clergy spouses and partners understand themselves as bound by a common faith or connected as individuals through that faith. Some follow a different faith tradition while others do not understand their marriage and union promises in primarily religious terms. Ways of understanding marriage and union with another view of marriage will be discussed in the following pages.

15. This behavior can also be seen in groups of pastors returning for continuing education events. Many are too tired and too preoccupied to extend even the most basic courtesy to those who serve their meals and clean their rooms.

Chapter Two

1. There are few who choose ordained ministry for professional reasons alone, but there are varying degrees of connection between personal faith and professional career choice. Ministry is rarely if ever a professional choice that has no basis in a personal faith and a sense of call. Amazingly, low pay, long hours, and emotionally charged work aren't appealing on their own!

2. This question is vital for those who share the same faith as their partner and equally important for those whose faith is different.

3. There are times when the faith journey of the nonordained partner takes precedence over that of the one seeking a professional call, but it is more common that the nonordained partner feels his or her faith is given up for the benefit of the other. If there are two faiths involved, this may be even more difficult.

4. This separation of experience may not occur if both partners are involved in leading worship, but it moves the experience from the personal to the professional realm.

5. The presence of children makes the matter of choosing a separate community or remaining in the community of call more complicated. This will be discussed in detail in subsequent pages.

6. In some cases, both partners make it clear before a call is taken that only the ordained half will be present in the ongoing life of the community.

7. The ordained partner is also experiencing this separation, but as an aspect of his or her vocation. The partner experiences the separation as personal.

8. The subject of PKs (preacher's kids) will be explored in much greater depth in later chapters.

Chapter Three

1. These quotes are taken from answers to a survey sent to the spouses and partners of ordained ministers. The survey was created specifically for this project. The participants' names are left out to preserve their privacy.

2. Michael Lane Morris and Priscilla White Blanton, "The Influence of Work-Related Stressors on Clergy Husbands and Their Wives," *Family Relations* 43 (April 1994): 189. Retirement and medical benefits as well as vacation time were considered in the overall assessment of compensation.

3. Morris and Blanton, "Influence," 191.

4. Ibid.

5. Ibid.. The levels of education of the clergy husbands were higher, with 75 persent holding graduate degrees. A Master's of Divinity is usually a prerequisite to ordained ministry in most denominations, so this is not surprising.

6. Morris and Blanton, "Influence," 191. They worked a mean of thirty-one hours per week and had worked for a mean of twenty-one years.

7. Morris and Blanton, "Influence," 192–93.

8. Ibid., 193.

9. Ibid.

10. In any covenant relationship, there should be equal say in the major decisions of the family. Unfortunately, this is not always the reality. Sometimes a paycheck brings with it the right to participate in making the decisions critical for the family.

11. Morris and Blanton, "Influence," 193–94.

12. In a longitudinal research survey for Episcopal Clergy Wellness conducted for Credo Institute, Inc., there were two interesting findings: male clergy tended to have higher levels of vocational satisfaction and financial self-efficacy than their female counterparts and were more likely to be in marriages or unions that supported self-efficacy. Female clergy reported higher levels of stress than their male counterparts. It would be a fruitful area of research to explore how the higher levels of stress for female clergy relate to their roles within the family. Those in unions or marriages and those who no longer have partners may be stressed because they face the same time constraint as the pastors' wives of the Morris and Blanton study. See *Clergy Wellness Report*, Credo Institute (June, 2006), 25–27, 30–31.

13. For those in same sex unions, even more gender issues arise. Discussing issues of sexuality and gender roles is uncomfortable for many individuals and communities. How this affects the covenant relationships of clergy and their partners is a vital area of research yet to be explored in any depth.

14. United Church of Christ, *Manual on Ministry: Perspectives and Procedures for Ecclesiastical Authorization of Ministry*, ucc.org/ministers/manual/.

15. This does not mean that an ordained person will continue to ask this question throughout life, but that it was seriously and prayerfully considered at least once.

16. For example, someone who works as a waiter may elaborate by remembering that providing food and drink creates a hospitable space for diners. The conversations had with a waiter may be the primary source of fellowship for some patrons.

17. Some of the gifts beyond professional ability to consider are hospitality, teaching, physical care, prophetic witness, the care of souls, and so on. These and others are gifts given to individuals for the benefit of everyone.

18. The spouse or partner may also want to answer these questions about their other half's ministry. Both may find that reviewing their work lives leads to a greater understanding of how they work together to deepen the lives of both, and of how they conflict and create tension.

19. For example, the income may sustain the family budget, allowing the ordained (and likely underpaid) ministry of the clergy half.

20. Many clergy take a position as an assistant for their first job. After two or three years, they move on to another church. After the first position, a minister may stay five years or more in a given location, depending upon the denominational expectations and the relationship with the church. In some denominations, assistant ministers are expected to resign if the senior pastor leaves. This can mean an unexpected and unwelcome job search and relocation.

21. One of the reasons for this is to make sure that the incoming minister has a chance to work without the presence of the previous minister getting in the way. It is also to make sure that members of a church do not leave the community to follow a particular pastor.

22. Morris and Blanton, "Influence," 191.

23. Morris and Blanton noted that the wives worked as teachers, secretaries, nurses, social workers, and business and sales clerks. These are professions that are found everywhere, making it easier to find work in each new location. Morris and Blanton, "Influence," 191.

24. Many pastors who find themselves unemployed due to a move work by filling in for vacationing ministers, work for short periods of time as interim pastors, or take positions in secular workplaces. Many denominations recognize the ordinations of ministers from other traditions, making it possible for pastors to serve churches outside their sponsoring denominations.

25. If there are no retirement plans available, this problem is even more complex. Unless the couple is able to save adequately for retirement without a plan attached to work, financial reality may favor one career taking priority over another.

26. This question becomes critical at certain points in the lives of children. It is very difficult for middle school and high school students to adjust to new schools, the loss of friends, and the difficulty of finding a new social group. Some towns may have schools that are unacceptable. If this is the situation, then private schools may be necessary, and their need to be expense factored into the family finances.

27. This question is especially critical for spouses or partners who do not work by choice, but work because their income is a financial necessity.

28. For example, do one or both partners wish to remain close to family, in specific geographical areas, or in particular types of environments (cities only, suburbs, small towns, rural areas)? These assumptions may go unstated but exercise great influence over which locations and careers are acceptable and which are not.

29. When family members require attention, this may be a critical factor. Are there ailing parents who require time and attention, or children who need more time than two careers allow? These factors may be important for a limited number of years, but should be included in the factors that affect career moves.

Chapter Four

1. These and other comments came from church members, clergy, and their spouses or partners.

2. The information about churches seeking ministers can be found through denominational sources as well as from the churches themselves. Churches seeking ministers often have pictures of the provided housing through a web site, giving the minister and spouse or partner a glimpse of the living space.

3. This leaves out the larger question of whether the couple feels called to live among people who make significantly more money, even if the education level is commensurate.

4. A couple could choose to send children to private schools if the public schools are not acceptable. This assumes there are private schools available and that the couple can afford to pay the tuition on their combined earnings.

5. Expectations about using the clergy housing for church business should not be based upon how the previous ministers acted, but upon how the present couple feels. Community members who feel called to offer the hospitality of their homes do so without communal pressure. The same should be true for the minister and spouse.

6. Sometimes, this issue is addressed before a minister takes a call to a specific church. During the interview process, the minister or the interviewing committee may bring up the subject so that no one is surprised afterward. If this issue is not addressed before accepting a call to serve a particular community, it should be addressed in the beginning weeks of the pastor's tenure.

7. In most instances, this allowance is exempt from federal tax. For this reason, clergy and their families must be aware of the tax laws that apply to clergy housing.

8. In some denominations, a minister's financial status is considered an aspect of his or her fitness for ministry. If he or she has debt that makes parish ministry or chaplaincy financially impossible, ordination and permission to serve a church may be delayed or refused. Some denominations and seminaries offer financial counseling so that an aspiring minster and his or her partner can avoid unreasonable debt.

9. If one or both partners will be working from home for a significant portion of the workweek, it should be considered when choosing the house location.

10. One couple was taken on a tour of the towns around a church. The guide noted the various elements in the towns, including this comment about one particular neighboring town: "You can live in any of these towns, but if you live in ________, we'll know you aren't one of us."

11. There may be special housing options for the minister and partner. In one case, a minister's family was able to rent a carriage house for a reasonable price on an estate near the church. Without this special arrangement, the family could not have afforded to live in that community.

12. This is true for children as well. Their achievements in school or other activities should not define them at home. They are first and foremost children of God and members of the family.

13. This time is not time to catch up on household chores, extra work, or other things on a never ending to-do list; this time is for the family to be together as a family, not just a collection of individuals who share a living space.

14. Each couple may want to have a list of situations that merit interrupting vacation or free time. Both should agree on these situations and should insist on preserving private time from other duties. Any vacation time lost to these situations should be taken at a later date.

15. As already mentioned, a list of expectations for the house and grounds that is approved by the couple and the church members makes the situation easier to address and correct. While it is within the community's right to object to mud wrestling on the front lawn, there should be no objections to a wading pool for children or having family and friends outside for a cookout. Both the community and the family must be reasonable.

16. There are some couples whose spotless homes reflect their own inner preferences and their fondness for cleaning, but they are the exception.

17. Some couples find it helpful to host a yearly open house, inviting all comers to their home. Others invite individuals or host specific events. However a couple interacts with their community or communities of faith, their actions should show care and hospitality toward others.

Chapter Five

1. Dan Cohn-Sherbok, *The Jewish Faith* (Valley Forge, Pa.: Trinity Press International, 1993), 162.

2. Ironically, lack of play can lead to diminished ability to work and reason because the mind never gets a time to rest. Originality of thought and action often requires the space for the mind to wander about, to play. For more on this, see the works of Bernard Lonergan, Robert Kegan, and Hans Georg Gadamer listed in the resources.

3. It's true that no one is delightful all the time. There are times when annoyance and irritation cloud enjoyment. Still, Sabbath play affirms that no one was put on this earth to accomplish as much as possible. At the most profound depth, people are on this earth to delight in God and each other. What comes out of that is blessed.

4. If family and friends create a stressful environment, the opposite may hold true: the couple feel more burdened and less connected to others.

5. If the spouse or partner is a member of a different faith community from that of the clergy half, he or she may have commitments on the weekends, too.

6. J. M. Darley and C. D. Batson conducted a "Good Samaritan" experiment with seminary students to see how time related to helping those in need. The results showed that the participants who were in a hurry did not stop to help someone in need as readily as the participants who were not in a hurry. This has profound implications for the overbooked lives of clergy and their partners. See the summary of this in Philip Zimbardo's *Psychology and Life*, 13th ed. (New York: Harper Collins, 1992), 594.

7. This does not mean that the clergy half becomes the "pastor" to his family. He or she is an equal member of this family faith community, not its leader or director. He or she is responsible equally with the spouse for fostering the faith lives of the family through play and prayer. The pastoral needs of the family should be addressed by an outside minister or ministers.

8. One option out of this either/or family dilemma is to choose to travel nowhere. Some couples opt to stay home for all holidays that involve worship services, inviting extended family to visit instead.

9. This will also work with typical school schedules. What it will not accommodate is extracurricular activities such as team sports. Whether the couple chooses a different Sabbath time or limits the number of activities that children can pursue on Sabbath days in a given year is up for discussion.

10. Many retired pastors continue to serve as interim ministers or fill in on Sundays for vacationing pastors. Some take the time to serve as mentors to those enter-

ing ministry, others join a specific church, helping out as needed. Many pastors could continue to preach and lead services every Sunday because of the demand for temporary or occasional clergy to supply the needs of churches.

Chapter Six

1. J. Gottman and N. Silver, *The Seven Principles for Making Marriage Work* (New York: Three Rivers Press, 2004).

2. Brent Atkinson, *Emotional Intelligence in Couples Therapy* (New York: W.W. Norton & Co., 2005). Atkinson's work goes well beyond what is described here, and he is considered to be at the cutting edge of therapy. He integrates the latest research from neurobiolgy into PET-C. Interested readers can read more about his work at http://thecouplesclinic.com/.

3. Paul Amato, David Johnson, Alan Booth, and Stacy Rogers, "Continuity and Change in Marital Quality between 1980 and 2000," *Journal of Marriage and Family* 65 (Feb. 2003): 1–22.

4. See William Doherty's excellent article, "How Therapy Can Be Hazardous to Your Marital Health," from the Smart Marriages Conference, July 3, 1999, available at http://www.smartmarriages.org/hazardous.html, for more details about this and tips for consumers.

5. S. M. Johnson, "Marital Problems," in *Effectiveness Research in Marriage and Family Therapy*, ed. D. Sprenkle, 163–90 (Alexandria, Va.: AAMFT, 2002).

6. T. P. Assay and M. J. Lambert, "The Empirical Case for the Common Factors in Therapy: Quantitative Findings," in *The Heart and Soul of Change: What Works in Therapy*, ed. M. A. Hubble, B. L. Duncan, and S. D. Miller, 35–36 (Washington, D.C.: APA Press, 1999).

7. E. S. Bordin, "The Generalizability of the Psychoanalytic Concept of the Working Alliance," *Psychotherapy: Theory, Research, and Practice* 16 (1979): 252–60.

8. J. Brown, S. Dreis, and D. K. Nace, "What Really Makes a Difference on Psychotherapy Outcome? Why Does Managed Care Want to Know?" in Hubble, Duncan, and Miller, eds., *The Heart and Soul of Change*, 389–406.

Chapter Seven

1. These comments are from a minister, a congregant, and a spouse.

2. This is true of many faiths because the parents begin knowing that they are responsible for fostering the spiritual life of their child—something that requires prayer, patience, and the ability to get out of God's way when necessary. At the same time, it relieves the parents of trying to control all aspects of their child's life—an idolatrous activity because only God envelops all of reality.

3. Unstructured play leads to a sharper mind, an active body, fewer behavioral issues, a greater imagination, and a deeper spiritual life. It is critical, but often forfeited in favor of structured activities. For more information on the importance of play in childhood development and spirituality, see the works of authors such as Jean Piaget, Hans Georg Gadamer, and Robert Kegan. Jerome Berryman's *Godly Play* makes the necessity for play, both physical and mental, a central tenet of Christian education. For difficult but interesting reading on this subject and its relation to faith and development, see James Loder's *The Logic of the Spirit: Human Development in Theological Perspective* (SanFrancisco: Jossey-Bass, 1998) and Gibson Winter's *Liberating Creation: Foundations of Religious Social Ethics* (New York: Crossroad, 1981).

4. The life's work of these authorities may be helpful: Erik H. Erikson, Dr. Benjamin Spock, Jean Piaget, Carol Gilligan, and Mary Pipher. For an informative look at these authors' ideas, among others, see Robert Kegan's *The Evolving Self: Problem and Process in Human Development* (Cambridge, Mass.: Harvard University Press, 1982).

5. Robert Coles's *The Spiritual Life of Children* (Boston: Houghton Mifflin, 1990, or other editions) is a classic text on the spiritual and moral lives of children. Jonathan Kozol's *Ordinary Resurrections* (New York: Crown Publishers, 2000) is a wonderful book about children, poverty, and education.

6. This is a difficult truth for most adults to accept and live into. Sadly, many adults spend their entire lives trying to earn love through their accomplishments. It is a legacy of fruitless suffering that many pass on to their children.

7. This is solid Christian theology, and is also developmentally sound. A child who is loved and valued in the present is a child who will be able to face the challenges of adulthood with a strong sense of self worth.

8. For an insightful discussion of this point, see Viktor Frankl's *Man's Search For Meaning* (Boston: Beacon Press, 2006), 150–53 in particular.

9. One PK who served as an acolyte in her father's church remarked that she never got the yearly thank-you letter that the other young acolytes received each June. She was expected to do the work without thanks because her father was a minister.

10. If the spouse or partner chooses to attend a different church from the one of the ordained half, he or she should let the clergy of the new church know that the children are trying to adjust to their new location. Leaders in the church can help a new child feel more welcome by making introductions and answering questions.

11. For a wonderful review of human development and the need to rebel from parents, see Kegan's *The Evolving Self.*

12. Other children are pressured to accept the family and community faith, but they do not have the added pressure of the parent's public ministry. These children may be pressured into public acceptance of faith, but it is rare that a parent's job is affected—or that the job affects the child's choice.

Chapter Eight

1. Mary, mother of Jesus, is told not to fear when she encounters God's messenger (Luke 1:30). The women who encountered God's messenger at Jesus' tomb were also told not to fear (Mark 16:6). An offering of peace is another way of saying "fear not"—see Jesus' reassurance for the disciples (Luke 24:36–40).

2. Divorce is never a good thing, but it is sometimes a necessary thing. When harm is inflicted and home life damaging to all concerned, it can be a life-saving step. There is no covenant if one or both partners are hurt physically, emotionally, or spiritually. An abusive situation is never something God intends.

3. When one or both work in fields that involve a lot of social interaction, it may be necessary to have a time of silence before engaging in conversation. Unless both are actively sharing and listening, it will not be a fruitful conversation. This can become a problem if the work of one partner is more isolating than socially engaging—that partner may have needs for verbal interaction that were met for the other half through social engagement at work.

4. *Book of Worship: United Church of Christ* (New York: UCC Office of Church and Life Leadership, 1986), 552.

BIBLIOGRAPHY

Liturgical Resources

The Book of Common Prayer. According to the use of the Episcopal Church. New York: Oxford University Press, 1990.

Book of Common Worship. Presbyterian Church (U.S.A.). Louisville: Westminster/John Knox Press, 1993.

Book of Worship: United Church of Christ. New York: Office of Church Life and Leadership, 1986.

Biblical and Theological Resources

Cohn-Sherbok, Dan. *The Jewish Faith*. Valley Forge, Pa.: Trinity Press International, 1993.

Hare, Douglas R. A. "Matthew." In *Interpretation: A Biblical Commentary for Teaching and Preaching*. Louisville: John Knox Press, 1993.

The Holy Bible (New Revised Standard Version). Nashville: Holman Bible Publishers, 1989.

O'Connor, M. "Judges." In *The New Jerome Biblical Commentary*. Englewood Cliffs, N.J.: Prentice Hall, 1990.

Willimon, William H. "Acts." In *Interpretation Series*. Louisville: John Knox Press. 1998.

Winter, Gibson. *Liberating Creation: Foundations of Religious Social Ethics*. New York: Crossroad, 1981.

Marriage Studies and Therapy Resources

Amato, Paul, David Johnson, Alan Booth, and Stacy Rogers. "Continuity and Change in Marital Quality between 1980 and 2000." *Journal of Marriage and Family* 65 (Feb. 2003): 1–22.

Assay, T. P., and M. J. Lambert. "The Empirical Case for the Common Factors in Therapy: Quantitative Findings." In *The Heart and Soul of Change: What Works in Therapy*, ed. M. A. Hubble, B. L. Duncan, and S. D. Miller, 35–56. Washington, D.C.: APA Press, 1999.

Atkinson, Brent. *Emotional Intelligence in Couples Therapy*. NewYork: W.W. Norton, 2005.

———. http://thecouplesclinic.com.

Bordin, E. S. "The Generalizability of the Psychoanalytic Concept of the Working Alliance." *Psychotherapy: Theory, Research, and Practice* 16 (1979): 252–60.

Brown, J., S. Dreis, and D. K. Nace. "What really makes a difference on psychotherapy outcome?" In *The Heart and Soul of Change: What Works in Therapy*, ed. M. A. Hubble, B. L. Duncan, and S. D. Miller, 389–406. Washington, D.C.: APA Press, 1999.

Gottman, J., and N. Silver. *The Seven Principles for Making Marriage Work*. NewYork: Three Rivers Press, 2004.

Johnson, S. M. "Marital Problems." In *Effectiveness Research in Marriage and Family Therapy*, ed. D. Sprenkle, 163–90. Alexandria, Va.: AAMFT, 2002.

Website Resources

www.AAMFT.org—a resource for licensed marriage and family therapists.

www.therapistlocator.net—a resource for locating licensed therapists.

www.thecouplesclinic.com—a user-friendly website with information on improving marriages.

Psychological and Educational Resources

Berryman, Jerome W. *Godly Play*. San Francisco: HarperSanFrancisco, 1991.

Coles, Robert. *The Moral Intelligence of Children: How to Raise a Moral Child*. New York: Plume, 1998.

———. *The Spiritual Life of Children*. Boston: Houghton Mifflin, 1990.

CREDO Institute. Clergy Wellness Report. June, 2006.

Daid, Robert Mace, and Vera Mace. *What's Happening to Clergy Marriages?* Nashville: Abingdon, 1980.

Darley, J. M., and C. D. Batson. "From Jerusalem to Jericho: A study of situational and dispositional variables in helping behavior," *Journal of Personality and Social Psychology* 27 (1973): 100–8.

Erikson, Erik. *Childhood and Society*. New York: W.W. Norton, 1963.

Frankl, Viktor. *Man's Search for Meaning*. Boston: Beacon Press, 2006.

Gadamer, Hans Georg. *Truth and Method (Wahrheit und Methode)*. New York: Crossroads, 1989.

Gilligan, Carol. *In A Different Voice: Psychological Theory and Women's Development*. Cambridge, Mass.: Harvard University Press, 1982, 1993 (3rd printing).

Hunt, Harley D., ed. *The Stained Glass Fishbowl: Strengthening Clergy Marriages*. Valley Forge, Pa.: Minister's Council, 1990.

Kegan, Robert. *The Evolving Self*. Cambridge: Harvard University Press, 1982.

———. *In over Our Heads: The Mental Demands of Modern Life*. Cambridge, Mass.: Harvard University Press, 1994.

Kindlon, Dan, and MichaelThompson. *Raising Cain: Protecting the Emotional Life of Boys*. New York: Ballantine Books, 1999.

Kozol, Jonathan. *Ordinary Resurrections: Children in the Years of Hope*. New York: Crown Publishers, 2000.

Loder, James. *The Logic of the Spirit: Human Development in Theological Perspective*. San Francisco: Jossey-Bass, 1998.

Lonergan, Bernard. *Insight: A Study of Human Understanding*. San Francisco: Harper & Row, 1978.

Morris, Michael Lane, and Priscilla White Blanton. "The Influence of Work-Related Stressors on Clergy Husbands and Their Wives." *Family Relations* (April 1994): 43.

Piaget, Jean. *The Child and Reality: Problems of Genetic Psychology*. New York: Penguin Books, 1976.

Piaget, Jean, and Barbel Inhelder. *The Psychology of the Child*. Trans. Helen Weaver. New York: Basic Books, 1969.

Pipher, Mary. *Reviving Ophelia: Saving the Selves of Adolescent Girls*. New York: Ballantine Books, 1994.

Rallings, E. M., and David J. Pratto. *Two-Clergy Marriages: A Special Case of Dual Careers*. Lanham, Md.: University Press of America,1984.

Sawtell, Peter S. *Clergy Couples in the United Church of Christ: A Statistical Survey*. Sioux City, Iowa, 1988. Not copyrighted.

Walrond-Skinner, Sue. *Double Bind: Clergy Marriages Since the Ordination of Women as Priests*. New York: Mowbray, 1998.

Zimbardo, Philip G. *Psychology and Life*. 13th ed. New York: Harper Collins, 1992.

Other Resources

Commission on Ministry. *Ordination Discernment Handbook 2006*. Episcopal Diocese of Massachusetts, 2006. Found on diocesan website: www.diomass.org.

Spock, Benjamin, MD. *Baby and Child Care*. Updated and revised by Robert Needlman, MD. New York: Pocket Books, 1998/2004.

Tidings. Monthly newsletter of St. Luke's Parish, Episcopal Church, Darien, Conn. View new editions at www.saintlukesdarien.org/tidings.html.

Webster, Richard M. "Primary Qualities for Professional Ministry." In Presbyterian Church (USA) SEIC Resource #92-102, "Study to Enrich Inquirers & Candidates," http://www.pcusa.org/prep4min/pdf/primary_qualities.pdf.

the relationship reflects this fact. There is no such thing as keeping a relationship the same when all of life moves forward. There is no going back to an earlier time in the relationship, except in memory. Life together changes the bond that continues to hold the couple together. This does not mean that the original relationship is lost, but it means that it must grow to accommodate the good and bad experiences, the arrival of new friends and family and the loss of loved ones, and the blessings and drawbacks of any given situation. The couple's relationship is placed in the larger context of life, lived out along with friends, family, faith community, and the wider world beyond the church doors. The complexity of it all can enhance daily life because the opportunities to see God's grace in life increase. The complexity can also drain happiness from daily life because it leads to more opportunities for loss and distraction.

Living into this complex and mutable relationship in a way that fosters the lives of both partners is not easy. It requires effort, time, and attention. Both must seek good things for their other half in how they live and in how they pray. The needs of self, the needs of the spouse or partner, and the needs of the larger family and community must be held together. The good of one partner cannot be pursued to the detriment of the other. This balancing of needs, this valuing of the lives of both, is difficult. The partners must have the courage to sacrifice for the other, the strength and trust to ask for the help and support of the other, and the patience to wait for the welfare of both to work out. A sense of humor can go a long way to making this adventure in partnership exciting rather than tedious. Prayer can reveal the sacred nature of the process and the reliability of God who holds both dear.

BEING HONEST WITH GOD, OURSELVES, AND OTHERS

Honesty may be the best policy, but that does not make it any easier to practice. It is a simple thing to hide the truth of personal identity. No spouse or partner is perfect, whether of the ordained or nonordained variety. It seems so inadequate to be the person God made and so much more appealing to create a self-sufficient shell to protect the all too vulnerable self. It is tempting to present this shell to one's partner, the world, and even to God. It is exhausting to maintain that shell. To let go of that perfect persona requires great trust—trust in the goodness and good-enoughness of self, trust in the